Teaching Early Reading
and Phonics

Education at SAGE

SAGE is a leading international publisher of journals, books, and electronic media for academic, educational, and professional markets.

Our education publishing includes:

- accessible and comprehensive texts for aspiring education professionals and practitioners looking to further their careers through continuing professional development

- inspirational advice and guidance for the classroom

- authoritative state of the art reference from the leading authors in the field

Find out more at: **www.sagepub.co.uk/education**

Teaching Early Reading and Phonics:

Creative Approaches to Early Literacy

Kathy Goouch and Andrew Lambirth

Los Angeles | London | New Delhi
Singapore | Washington DC

First published 2011

SAGE Publications Ltd
1 Oliver's Yard
55 City Road
London EC1Y 1SP

SAGE Publications Inc.
2455 Teller Road
Thousand Oaks, California 91320

SAGE Publications India Pvt Ltd
B 1/I 1 Mohan Cooperative Industrial Area
Mathura Road
New Delhi 110 044

SAGE Publications Asia-Pacific Pte Ltd
33 Pekin Street #02-01
Far East Square
Singapore 048763

Library of Congress Control Number 2010924372

British Library Cataloguing in Publication data

A catalogue record for this book is available from the British Library

ISBN 978-1-84920-421-7
ISBN 978-1-84920-422-4 (pbk)

Typeset by C&M Digitals (P) Ltd, Chennai, India
Printed in Great Britain by MPG Books Group, Bodmin, Cornwall
Printed on paper from sustainable resources

Mixed Sources
Product group from well-managed
forests and other controlled sources
www.fsc.org Cert no. SA-COC-1565
© 1996 Forest Stewardship Council
FSC

Dedication

We would like to dedicate this book to the many children, teachers, academics and authors from whom we have learned.

We would also like to acknowledge those teachers whose professionalism continues to be guided and nourished by research, scholarship and the pursuit of truth.

Contents

List of abbreviations

APP	Assessment of Pupil Progress
CLPE	Centre for Literacy in Primary Education
CPA	cognitive psychological approach
DCSF	Department for Children, Schools and Families
DEAR	Drop Everything and Read
DfEE	Department for Education and Employment
DfES	Department for Education and Skills
HMI	Her Majesty's Inspectorate
NAAE	National Association of Advisors in English
NATE	National Association for the Teaching of English
ORT	Oxford Reading Tree
PIRLS	Progress in International Reading Literacy Study
PISA	Program for International Student Assessment
SQUIRT	Sustained Quiet Uninterrupted Independent Reading Time
UKLA	UK Literacy Association
USSR	Uninterrupted Sustained Silent Reading

1

Sensible approaches to the teaching of reading

In this chapter we aim:

- to draw together research and practice in the teaching of reading;
- to introduce reading as a complex activity;
- to also describe the teaching of reading as complex;
- to claim that the broad and diverse range of children's early experiences needs to be acknowledged, celebrated and used as a foundation for new learning.

The book

In 2007 we felt very strongly that there was a need to publish research information in relation to the teaching of reading and in support of teachers who were struggling to understand phonics and its place in their pedagogy (Goouch and Lambirth 2007b). This followed a very crowded and enthusiastic conference when teachers, advisors and academics gathered together to challenge the findings of the interim report of the Rose Review (2006). While there had been a plethora of government material instructing teachers about the teaching of reading, there appeared to us then, and now, to be very few voices heard challenging the prevailing phonics discourse and even fewer books available offering a critical perspective. This was particularly the case following the publication of the final version of the Rose Review (2006). We gathered together the work from a number of renowned academics for the purpose of offering a critical and research-informed text about how children learn to read and how we can best help them. Subsequently, in our conversations with teachers and students at all levels, we find there is also a hunger for this research information to be helpfully translated into practice guidance. This book is our attempt to fulfil that requirement. We find, however, that we are unable to offer simple practice guides without reference to the research to support such work and so readers will not find this book devoid of references to theory, research and scholarship in the field and clear connections between research and practice. In fact, our belief in the teaching community is such that we feel confident that when they read our brief 'pointers' towards practice in this text they will creatively and competently set their planning and practice paths in the right direction, that is the direction best serving children, rather than methods or programmes, politics or policy.

For decades now debates have raged around us about the method of teaching reading thought to be most appropriate, often resulting in 'absolutism and dogmatism' (Hannon 2000: 71) as can be seen in recent dictats from central government and some of the lobbyists surrounding recent initiatives. In an early work Meek suggested that phonics was popular as a teaching procedure because 'insecure or inexperienced teachers find it one they can both understand and administer', persevering with it because 'in our imperfect world it seems to be the most efficient system we have yet devised for beginners' (1982: 74–5). But however seductive some of the apparently new simple views seem to be, it is commonly acknowledged that there can be no 'one size fits all' approach. This is obviously disappointing for busy and anxious teachers who now find that every aspect of current political dogmatism is available as a downloadable, often free, printable resource. In this book we will try to help by being clear that there are different and alternative approaches to teaching young children to read. While including phonics as one element of reading development, our approach is not dominated by this nor does it view decoding print as an end in itself. Instead, this way of thinking about teaching reading is centred upon the much more important aspect of making meaning, with phonics as one tool that might be useful to some children in the process of learning to read.

Recent history

We will not dwell too much on the history of the debates relating to the teaching of reading, in existence even before the famous Bullock Report (1975) which set out so clearly its recommendations that children should learn to read in context, that 'language should be learned in the course of using it in, and about, the daily experiences of the classroom and the home' (p. 520) and not through the use of formal exercises and drilling. This report was exceptional in three other ways. It acknowledged the potential gulf between research and teaching and sought to remedy what it called 'this uneasy relationship' by recommending teachers' involvement with research and researchers' involvement with teaching. In addition, it made its recommendations on the basis of research findings, broadly gathered and carefully considered. Finally, it sought to seriously unravel the complexities involved in children learning to read and in teachers teaching reading. It is always important to acknowledge the political context within which current central government reports are written and in which initiatives relating to phonics are situated. In the middle of the 1970s there were raging debates about the overemphasis on creativity and creative approaches in the classroom. The case is similar today and similar groups are powerful lobbyists. The current demand for simple solutions and easily measurable test results does not come from parents, teachers or children. It comes instead from politicians and those involved in commercial enterprises, both groups it could be argued who have limited information about how children develop as readers. Both groups can also be seen to benefit from quick wins, easy targets and the play on parents' emotions to gain rapid success for their children. In addition it is also important to realise that, while England appears to be quite separate in its approach from other countries in the United kingdom, it is very close to other English-speaking countries across the world, and in particular approaches being taken in some parts of the United States (see, for example, the work of Shannon 2007).

The research

The Rose Review has already been mentioned but it is important to be clear about this document and its relevance for this book. This Review is actually named the *Independent Review of the Teaching of Early Reading* but rather than being independent in any sense, it was commissioned by the government in 2005. It is also interesting to note that, although 'early reading' features in the title, the Review focuses its attention almost entirely on phonics from its opening summary page where the second sentence talks about Her Majesty's Inspectorate (HMI) finding phonics teaching to be a neglected or weak feature of teaching (with no accompanying reference) to the clear statement in the Aspects listed as the remit for the Review; here it states that the Review has examined and commented upon 'what best practice should be expected in the teaching of early reading and synthetic phonics' (p. 7).

Evidently there was no attempt made at 'independence' in this Review nor any pretence at it being less than partial towards a particular aspect of reading and a particular model of phonics instruction. The Review was commissioned and reported at a time when teacher professionalism had already been challenged, if not eroded, by the National Strategies (DfEE 1998) (see, for example, Frater 2000; Messenheimer and Packwood 2002; Bryan 2004) and teachers were therefore much more likely to succumb to persuasion from national governmental sources (Hall 2004). The Bullock Report cited earlier founded its conclusions and recommendations upon wide-ranging research evidence and famously called for teachers to gather greater insight into educational research (1975: 554). The Rose Review offered completely the reverse perspective:

> While robust research findings must not be ignored, developers of national strategies, much less schools and settings, cannot always wait for the results of long-term research studies. They must take decisions, based on as much firm evidence as is available from a range of sources at the time, especially from replicable and sustainable best practice. (2006: 15)

The conclusions drawn from the Rose Review have now become embedded within the Early Years Foundation Stage, a statutory document since 2007 in England. It is not the task of this book to trawl once more through and challenge the basis and the findings of the Rose Review; this has been robustly achieved in a number of other texts (see, for example, Hynds 2007; Rosen 2006; UKLA, undated submission to the Rose Review). Instead, it is possible to identify a small number of research reports that indicate that children's learning, and in particular learning about reading, is complex and often unsystematic. Here in England researchers have identified that children are intentional learners, curious and keen from birth to make sense of their world and to identify patterns around them to help in this sense-making (Hall 2006; David et al. 2003). Learning language, both spoken and written, is culturally framed before and outside of school and 'best practice' often involves recognising literacy practices in homes and communities and creating bridges between these experiences and new learning. Although many researchers agree that knowledge of the alphabetic principle is an essential component in learning to read, it is difficult to understand why it could be assumed that this should be learned in isolation, that is, separate from meaning-making or comprehension as it is sometimes referred to. In the US, Strauss and Altwerger analyse and report empirical research carried out there which absolutely refutes any suggestion that 'intensive, systematic phonics programmes are … superior to literature-based programmes in developing students' decontextualised phonics skills or contextualised use of phonics cues' (2007: 216). In fact, the research found that the higher the phonic scores of children (more than 100) in the study, the lower their ability to retell and, conversely, the best retellers had the lowest phonic scores. In fact, what many research studies seem to be reporting is that good readers pay the least attention to the phonemic level of print.

The politics

In 2006 and 2007, the UK government decided to act upon the Rose Review and ensure that its recommendations were enshrined in statutory documentation to enforce the 'phonics first and fast' approach to teaching reading. As we now know, the report and thus the ensuing compliant practice was heavily influenced by lobbyists, with critics such as Wray, Barrs and Meek Spencer worrying about from where the government's information has emerged:

> There's no question that lobby groups such as the Reading Reform Foundation and the Dyslexia Association have had a disproportionate amount of influence on government educational policies. (Barrs and Meek Spencer 2007: 162)

> Government ministers and Rose himself try to dress the report's recommendations as based on a consensus derived from research. This is actually nonsense. What has actually happened is that pressure groups with axes to grind (and, actually teaching programmes to sell) have caught the ear of politicians and the Rose Review was never going to be a balanced interpretation of the evidence. (Wray 2006: 128)

Also, it seems that the government has been hugely successful in swaying public opinion toward a so-called common-sense approach, reducing reading to phoneme recognition and a functional level. The choices of whose information is to be trusted to inform government policy are interesting here and mirror the ways that similar decisions seem to have been made in the USA (for example, see Shannon 2007). But why would a government enshrine practice in law that is neither informed by high-quality research nor by educationalists, including teachers? From the government's own statistics we know that in 2008 86 per cent of children achieved Level 4 or above in the Key Stage 2 reading test; 83 per cent of boys achieved Level 4 or above and 89 per cent of girls. We also know that these statistics have barely changed between 2000 and 2008 (DCSF Standards). While it is important to note that this would mean that there may be 11 per cent of girls and 17 per cent of boys who did not achieve Level 4 or above, this does not necessarily mean that the same figures are unable to read. It may mean that they were unable to perform at that level on the day, with the particular kind of task, they may be reading at Level 3 or they may not have been present at school to be tested. It remains though that on the basis of such statistics – however they are read and interpreted and understood – all children in England are now being subjected to a 'uni-dimensional approach to the teaching of a multi-dimensional process' (Wray 2006: 128) and that the new approach is informed by psychologists and others with perhaps a vested interest beyond that of the success of all children learning to read.

It is interesting that now, a few years along the road since 'phonics first and fast' became the mantra from policy-makers and politicians and commercial publishers in England, a spokesman for the DCSF is reported as saying that 'phonics was never intended as a quick fix' (Scott 2010). Importantly, Clackmannanshire, which is the authority in Scotland upon which Professor Rose based much of his review recommendations, is reported as having the view that 'synthetic phonics in itself was not a magic bullet'. 'We would see it as an important component of learning to read, but it is not the only component. That's the difference between Scotland and England' (Scott 2010). In the same report, the Head of West Dunbartonshire Council (another heavily-cited local authority used by those supporting a synthetic phonics 'one size fits all' approach and informants to the Rose Review) claim that synthetic phonics was only 'one strand in a 10-step programme which included extra time in the curriculum for reading, home support for parents and the fostering of a "literacy environment" for reading'. It is interesting also to note that in Scotland 18.5 per cent of children are reported to leave primary school 'functionally illiterate'. To summarise, in the government's review headed by Professor Rose, those areas of Scotland which were claimed as beacons shining light on the importance of synthetic phonics first, fast and only are not doing so and may never have done so. In addition, while Scotland was hailed as having 'a tradition of teaching phonics which almost certainly continued over a period when it had fallen out of favour in England' (Rose 2006: n223) it is also struggling with some persistent statistics which seem to reflect that there remains a small group of children who are not succeeding in learning to read at even a basic level. Even the term 'functional literacy' is contentious. One definition of being functionally literate is 'if [they] are able to engage effectively in all of those activities in which literacy is normally assumed in their culture or group' (Barton 1994: 193). The assumption made in government statistics and discussions is that there is a homogenous literacy culture to which we all belong. We are now clear of course that this is not the case and that it is not possible to assume a single, common literacy standard but rather acknowledge the range of literacies in which children/people engage.

Most education scholars would acknowledge that phonics has a part to play in the support of children's development as readers but the part it plays in learning to read and in reading is the focus of the debate. If the act of reading is defined very narrowly in simple measurable terms (see, for example, Stainthorpe 2006: 117) then the act of cracking the alphabetic code is often seen to be central to this. If, however, reading is acknowledged as being a complex process 'based on several different kinds of knowledge, and their learning to read was a matter of learning to draw on all these sources of information in the act of reading' (Barrs and Meek Spencer 2007: 151) then simply providing children with phoneme recognition skills is in danger of disadvantaging children, misleading them as to the complexity of the English language and disaffecting children at the earliest stages who will not see the advantage of learning sounds. Far from Stainthorpe's claim that 'if they are taught the letter–sound correspondence and how to blend sounds into words, they are armed with a strategy for reading words independently ... if children have this knowledge they have a necessary tool for developing fluent word reading' (2006: 117), we would claim that such narrow teaching *disarms* children, *misleads* them about how the English language is represented symbolically and importantly *misdirects* them about the very nature of reading. This book is founded on the belief that by 'putting children's meaning-making at the heart of their learning' (Meek Spencer 2007: 164) and acknowledging the volitional nature of learning – and particularly literacy learning – and the efficacy of social constructivist approaches (Hall 2006), children will be more closely engaged with their learning, motivated to learn and supported by teachers who not only understand them as learners but also understand the nature of reading and how children learn to read.

The practice

Children are different and may learn differently. Further, children in any one class will arguably have had a diverse range of early experiences in literacy, phonological support and letter/sound introductions. While most teachers are aware of this, many still engage in practices that they themselves were familiar with as children, particularly now that the government, via Professor Rose, the National Strategies and the Early Years Foundation Stage, has imposed a one-size-fits-all programme for teachers to follow (Primary National

Strategy 2007). Some of us, however, have real teachers' anecdotes to help our understanding and in support of empirical research. One colleague whooped for joy as she came into the staffroom at lunchtime, full of joy at the fact that one child had 'cracked it' – not with phonic programmes, nor with phonic games, nor with phonically regular texts (the 'decodable books' referred to in the Rose Review which promotes so-called 'quick wins' (n82)) – but with *Bringing the Rain to Kapiti Plain* (Aardema 1986). This is a story based on an African legend with strong rhyme and a strong pattern to help developing readers. Listen to just one part of this engaging text:

> These are the cows, all hungry and dry,
>
> Who mooed for the rain to fall from the sky;
>
> To green-up the grass, all brown and dead,
>
> That needed the rain from the cloud overhead –
>
> The big black cloud, all heavy with rain,
>
> That shadowed the ground on Kapiti Plain.

In this, there are few phonically regular worlds (e.g. 'big') but having heard the story, enjoyed it, shared it with others, drawn pictures about it, enjoyed role play from it, played with it – on this day, this five-year-old boy read it with accuracy, fluency, understanding, enjoyment and pride. What must he be learning from his persistence with this text in relation to the content, the richness of the vocabulary, the tune on the page, as well as the absolute sense of achievement in orchestrating the decoding of print and clear comprehension of the content? This text, like all good books, opened another world to him and motivated him towards new reading experiences and other worlds. Compare this with:

> The sheep is shut in the pen. The grass is green. The sun shines. We will
>
> Let the sheep out now. We will grow if the sun shines. The sun is hot today.
>
> I have lost my shoe in the steep street. It had a crown on it. I will get it.
>
> (SND, *c*. 1920)

It is this on this kind of antiquated meaningless text that new 'decodable' books are now being based (see, for example, the new Floppy's Phonics from the Oxford Reading Tree and Bob Bug from the new Songbirds phonics titles from ORT). Such texts are a far cry from the meaning-packed *Bringing the Rain to Kapiti Plain*, with all its subdued references and the possibility of connections to be made and considered. The tune of its text of course will be familiar to young children from timeless nursery rhymes and the memorable, 'This is the House that Jack Built'. I can hear critics lining up to decry this as anecdotal and therefore irrelevant in a research argument. My point is that the teaching world is packed full of such anecdotes – just ask teachers. Meek of course constructed the seminal work *How Texts Teach What Readers Learn* (1988) decades ago in the knowledge that it is not teachers alone or programmes that make a difference but the human connection between reader and text and teacher that consistently provides the reading lesson.

What seems to be important to remember is that phonics is not *an end* in itself, whether it be synthetic or any other kind of phonics. Further, reading is also not always an end in itself but often a beginning, a pathway to other worlds, other learning and affirmation or challenge to our own worlds. Neither can phonics be allowed to be *the beginning* of learning to read. Many children receive reading lessons long before starting school in the form of shared texts that are written, told or read, and it has been estimated that some children may have received 6,000 stories before starting school (Barton 1994). Thankfully, legislation cannot impinge on these reading lessons. These children will have a head start when they begin school with their knowledge of how stories work, patterns and tunes in stories, the relationship between illustration and print as well as some clear information about print drawn from reading and re-reading favourite tales. The children with this kind of rich early literacy experience (Goouch 2007) will mostly be able to withstand reductionist reading tuition when they start school, though some may become disaffected. Those children, however, who have not had the benefit of mediated early experiences in a range of literacy and reading practices before they start school in this current era of prescriptive practice will find their first reading lessons to be the recounting of sounds rather than the joy of tuning into meaning in encounters with high-quality books and stories.

It is easy to make young children recount sounds, to chant together, to take part in phonics games, to copy letters on 'sound' worksheets. Young children are mostly compliant and eager to please. We are though, as their reading teachers, completely unable to *make* children form connections, to *make* them understand, to *make* them learn to read. As Hall makes clear, 'accomplished reading teachers ... see their learners as intentional beings and ... see learning itself as a volitional process' (2006: 20). We cannot make children learn to read. We can, however, entice them, make reading a pleasurable experience, invite them into story worlds, create affective opportunities for children to participate in reading, provide space and resources for children to play with stories, join in with them in playing with the sounds of the stories, help them to find tunes and patterns in print, immerse them in the pleasurable sounds of our language – delicious onomatopoeic and alliterative examples are frequently found in good picture fiction (see, for example, *We're Going on a Bear Hunt* and *Mr Gumpy's Motor Car*). And within these writing, talking, listening and reading experiences we can also help children to make sense of the alphabetic code.

Using phonics as a core method to teach reading *is* seductive as it appears simple and efficient, with letters and sounds to be ticked off by teachers when they have been memorised. In reality, reading is not simple and neither is learning sounds in our language (Goswami 2007; Goswami and Bryant 1990), and our preoccupation with efficiency and quick wins in reading is in contrast with the efficacy of the teaching in other nations and cultures where children at the age of four and five are not at school receiving reading instruction but are playing at home or in kindergartens. The results of this sound beginning to learning are clearly evident in international statistics (see Mullis et al. 2006).

Quick wins and efficiency, systematic approaches and incremental learning belong to the language of politics where short-term goals are important and easily measurable outcomes are the basis of popular headlines and soundbites. In classrooms, children make life slightly more complex as their learning progress is often messy rather than systematically secure and learning happens over time rather than as a single event as children make connections with prior learning, often outside of school, and across contexts and subject barriers.

Although it has been claimed that when children learn to read the 'language of written texts is accessed via the eyes rather than the ears' (Rose 2006: appendix, n62), those of us working with children as teachers and parents, rather than laboratory scientists, know that this simple explanation is not the case. Children become attuned to texts; they learn the tunes and language of texts which is why multi-sensory approaches are often successful as discussed above. In addition, we also know from the work of neuroscience and now neuroimaging that brain activity during reading occurs in different brain regions with connections being made across those regions as we both decode and experience words (Price 2000). This makes the idea of children using only their eyes rather than their ears to access print somewhat oversimplistic.

Conclusion

In this chapter we have introduced the context for this new book in a number of ways. We have stated our aim – which is to provide a research-informed text for teachers which will also include ideas to connect theory with their practice. We have stated our view that the politics and policy context for the move towards synthetic phonics only practice is in danger of leading towards a damaging reductionist approach to the teaching of reading, described by Meek as 'a thinner gruel of educational nourishment' (1987: viii) in its attempts to construct reading as simply being able 'to come to terms with the alphabetic principles if they are to learn to read and write' (Rose 2006: 16). We have begun to construct reading in this chapter as a complex, social and cultural activity, with lessons often learned in the first instance in multi-dimensional family and outside-school contexts and from a range of texts, including print texts. We have begun in this chapter to also construct learning as being a broader and more sophisticated activity than simply listening to instruction, and learners as volitional and sophisticated themselves in their abilities to draw information from a range of sources in a relatively short space of time and from a range of places in order to become readers at varying developmental stages by the time they make their first school encounters with literacy.

Finally...

In this book we are writing for teachers who are not satisfied with, as Stannard describes it, 'the Stainthorpe and Stuart' model (Stannard 2006: 121) but are looking instead for alternatives. Teachers generally are rather conservative and very compliant but above all teachers work hard as they seek to help children to learn, and hopefully this book will help them to achieve this objective. In Chapter 2, 'Critical contexts', the theoretical background to this book is fully and critically reviewed and includes examination of the Rose Review as well as the Early Years Foundation Stage. Chapter 3 is a discussion of 'The role of the teacher'. In this chapter, knowledge for teaching and the theoretical arguments relating to how teachers teach is illustrated by practical suggestions on how connections can be forged between theory and practice in principled classroom activities. In Chapter 4, 'Knowledge for reading', the knowledge required by children to ensure their development as readers is outlined and discussed. In this chapter, what children need to know, experience and understand is carefully presented with ways to embed important alphabetic information into real and meaningful activities and texts. An effective environment for reading is proposed in Chapter 5, 'Environments for reading', with ideas about what a print-rich environment could actually look like presented in practical terms. To follow this, in Chapter 6, 'Resources for reading', the kinds of resources that children need in order to experience a rich literacy curriculum and the kinds of high-quality texts required is described with the emphasis clearly on children's literature. 'Reading routines' is the focus of Chapter 7, in which we argue that there are a range of regular activities that are absolutely essential to support children's reading development. 'Talk, reading and writing', in Chapter 8 makes links between classroom activities involving talk, reading and writing and we suggest that the three modes of language are closely interconnected in effective literacy classrooms. In Chapter 9, 'Assessment of reading', we draw together ideas for creative and critical pedagogy and also address the important issue of assessment and how children's reading can most usefully be described and recorded. A summary is offered in Chapter 10, 'Conclusions: principles and practice', and here we present what we believe to be 'the non-negotiable principles and elements of effective practice in literacy in primary education'. We claim in this final chapter that the approaches recommended and illustrated in this book will lift children's experience of learning to read and to be literate beyond contemporary politically and commercially motivated emphases which threaten to limit professional creativity and integrity.

Further reading

Goouch, K. and Lambirth, A. (2007) *Understanding Phonics and the Teaching of Reading: Critical Perspectives*. Maidenhead: Open University Press/McGraw-Hill.
Hall, K. (2004) *Literacy and Schooling: Towards Renewal in Primary Education Policy*. Aldershot: Ashgate Publishing Ltd.

Critical contexts

In this chapter we aim:

- to describe how forms of reading pedagogy are based upon ideology and are informed by a tradition of research and scholarship;
- to explain that humans are a symbolic species and that learning to use written words extends our symbolic communicative repertoires;
- to discuss the view that literacy learning requires active participation and collaboration and does not begin in school;
- to introduce cognitive psychological perspectives that often demand that children are taught specific skills on a linear and staged path through instruction.

Every classroom in every school betrays a theory of learning. The teaching in schools owes a debt to a philosophy of education. None of this is 'just common sense'; everything can be traced back to an ideological stance towards the education and schooling of children. How reading is taught in schools is no different. This book makes known our theoretical and, consequently, ideological approach to the teaching of reading. Our views have been further honed and enriched by our combined teaching experience of over fifty years. Understanding reading and how it should be taught is complex and sometimes difficult. However, the rewards for one's intellectual efforts to understand the processes are rich. So we make no apologies for believing in the academic stamina of our readership as well as a will to learn more practical ideas. In this chapter we offer an overview of the theoretical background of the approach to this book. It will begin with what we perceive to be important insights into how children develop to be competent language users, both oral and written. We believe the position on early language acquisition is the foundation to further perspectives on reading pedagogy and the relevance of the teaching of phonics. We will go on to examine alternative views to our own position in the form of what has been called 'cognitive psychological approaches' (CPAs) (Hall 2003: 53), whose perspectives have attained a favourable position with contemporary policy-makers across the western world and have led to significant changes to curricula. In England, the most influential manifestation of cognitive psychological approaches has been the *Independent Review of the Teaching of Early Reading* (Rose 2006) which has subsequently infused other crucial curriculum documentation like the *Early Years Foundation Document* (DCFS 2007). We will introduce and attempt to critique both documents, drawing on research and scholarship from around the world. Lastly, utilising this research, we will discuss what we consider to be the 'basics' of reading pedagogy.

Language acquisition

Humans have been described as a 'symbolic species' (Deacon 1997). This means that we let things represent other things. We can do this through the use of our language. Language is not only a mode of communication; it is the expression of a rare form of thought – symbolic representation. Deacon (1997) writes that:

> Though we share the same earth with millions of kinds of living creatures, we also live in a world that no other species has access to. We inhabit a world full of abstractions, impossibilities, and paradoxes ... We tell stories about our real experiences and invent stories about imagined ones, and even make use of these stories to organise our lives. In a real sense, we live our lives in this shared virtual world. And slowly, over the millennia, we have come to realise that no other species on earth seems able to follow us into this miraculous place. (p. 22)

The unique way that human language can represent the world – objects, events and relationships – facilitates an infinite variety of representations and a powerful means of predicting, organising memories and planning actions (Deacon 1997). This form of representation of the world shapes our thinking and the ways in which we know our reality. Our acquisition and our uses of language are natural, honed by thousands of years of evolution, and are inseparable from our intelligence. As teachers, our understanding of general human abilities and the awe-inspiring phenomena of human intelligence and mental capability should direct our approach to curricula and pedagogy. As we begin to realise our role as mediators of a culture and nurturers of young minds, we recognise that teaching in schools has no place for amateurs or ill-informed technicians; it is a position for fully informed, creative professionals.

Human language learning is *'both personal and social'* (Goodman 1996: 117–25). We need language for our own thoughts and learning, but we also need to use it to engage with the culture and community around us for survival and development. The linguist Chomsky (1972) puzzled over how children as young as four seem implicitly to know an enormous amount about complex grammatical rules and their application, without any kind of teaching – indeed this form of knowledge is arguably far too complex for children to learn in any formal way. Chomsky contends that a child's incredible feat of learning results from some kind of 'innate competence'. He suggests that there exists an innate universal grammar. Although languages look incredibly variable, they do in fact share a deep common logic from which the specific rules used by each can be derived by the use of a kind of deductive logic. This grammatical knowledge is not given, therefore it must reside as innately known rules. As some have pointed out (Deacon 1997; Pinker 1994), the theory has come about through a strong will to come to terms with these processes but as yet no one has been able to prove the existence of this innate device for learning language. Yet there is no doubt that there is something special about the human brain that enables us to learn a language without any form of teaching in the normal sense of the word. What this also means is that language is not learned in the same way as other things like learning to walk or like the learning of other animals, it is 'personal and social'. This is an important point to consider for teachers in school. It suggests that something other than 'instruction' may need to be used when we are dealing with a phenomenon as fundamental as language learning. It is natural to human beings to learn a language and to symbolically represent the world. This, therefore, should dictate the environments for learning we strive to create in schools.

Goodman (1996) is described as being a psycholinguist in his approach. He, Yetta Goodman and Frank Smith (1973) led the way in applying this nativist approach to oral language acquisition to learning about written language. Their ideas have had an enormous influence on teachers' understanding of learning to read, including our own.

Goodman (1996) contends that written language is learned later in life, after oral language, but is in no way less natural than oral language acquisition. He argues that both

> develop out of the need of humans to think symbolically and to communicate in a growing range of contexts and functions, as individuals and as societies. Written language is an extension of human language development that occurs when it's needed: when face-to-face and here-and-now language is no longer sufficient. (pp. 117–25)

This position for the naturalness and similarity of learning oral language and learning to use the written word is often criticised for misunderstanding the evolutionary development of the human brain and its relationship to language. Humans have used oral language for thousands of years – there has been time for the human mind to evolve to produce internal mechanisms to assist the acquisition of language – but written language is a relatively new tool and therefore it has not had the time to become natural and intrinsic to the brain's construction. However, Goodman is clear that learning written language is natural because humans are a uniquely symbolic species – we need to learn to think symbolically and to communicate through language in multiple ways. Written language extends our symbolic communicative repertoires – it is natural in so far as it is natural to have the capacity to read and to write. We would want to add that learning to read and write also happens to be a cultural process (Lave and Wenger 1991; Rogoff 1990). In basic terms, this means that there are some things within a culture that are considered so important that a society ensures that everyone who needs to, learns to do it (Gee 2004). Boosting one's communicative repertoires to include the use of the printed word is vital for modern societies to function and prosper – reading and writing have a huge cultural significance.

So far in this chapter, we have presented the work of scholars and scientists who have shown that humans are a symbolic species, who naturally and uniquely among the animal world acquire the means to represent the world symbolically. Human beings' capacity to learn a language and the fundamental, personal and social nature of this language acquisition means that we learn it in a different way than we do other things. Oral language and written language are different forms of a communicative repertoire that exist around the use of language. Yet, as Goodman points out, oral and written language are both symbolic forms of communication and therefore we must recognise that they are learned in similar ways. If we agree with these ideas, then how we encourage or teach children about language – like reading – needs to be considered very carefully, questioning the more formal kinds of instruction that a good deal of contemporary reading pedagogy exploits.

Joining the dots of learning theory and reading pedagogy

It was the psychologist Bruner (1960, 1996), drawing on the work of Vygotsky (1978) who said knowledge is the product of 'making'. In other words: 'Discovery ... is possible only by constructing understandings on the basis of extensions, elaborations or reformulations of current or preceding understandings' (Olson 2001: 105). Children's acquisition of knowledge is made by reorganising what they already know about the world. This is a 'constructivist' approach to learning, which states that knowledge is made or constructed by the learner in their own terms.

As with other theoretical positions discussed earlier in this chapter, one has to decide about the validity of this position. Other theories of learning, like behaviourism, are in fundamental opposition to the ideas of constructivism but influence reading pedagogy, particularly the teaching of synthetic phonics. How we teach reading must be led by learning theory. This is what we mean by 'joining the dots of learning theory and reading pedagogy'. In this book we have been heavily influenced by the ideas of Bruner (1960, 1996) and constructivism and this sculpts our approach to the teaching of reading. Understanding that we learn by drawing on our internal models of the world and restructuring, extending and reformulating them in the light of new knowledge will influence what we know about learning language, both oral and written.

In connection with this constructivist perspective, it is important to recognise that literacy learning does not begin in school (Street and Street 1991). Children come to school, already rich in literacy experiences (Goodman 1996). Many children already have begun to make sense of print at home and many parents, often unwittingly, follow and support their development (Halliday 1975). However, literacy has been said to have been 'pedagogised' by successive contemporary education policies (Street and Street 1991) – this is when a particular form of literacy and language learning is promoted and taught in school in a reified way. This creates the impression that literacy is uniquely acquired in school through a process of instruction and where one is tested to ascertain how much of it we have learned. We, the writers of this book, always find it strange when we hear children confess that they are 'not good at literacy'. But we know the capacity for language acquisition is a natural process and that language use and literacy events occur all the time inside and outside school. Pedagogisation of language acquisition and literacy can have the effect of alienating children from their own language – convincing some children that they are 'not good' at either acquiring it or using it.

Schools should not make the mistake of believing that what they are teaching children is entirely new (Goodman 1996). Instead, teachers need to build upon the beginnings that children have already made in language. This is not to suggest that schools have nothing to offer – on the contrary, there is much to teach and to learn about language, its forms, its power and its affordances in society, but children's already considerable knowledge about language needs to be given validity. Children have been surrounded by print since they were born and begin to respond to it very early on. Slowly, they begin to take control of the written system of language. Children's play becomes imbued with written language – they make notes, write cards to friends and family and play at reading books. As the subsequent chapters of this book will describe, teachers take advantage of this emerging literacy and create a culture within the classroom that facilitates experiences with texts and builds directly on these early foundations.

Learning and changing participation

The notion of children's learning from home and outside school being utilised in classrooms by teachers was extended by Rogoff (2003) with what she called a socio-cultural-historical theory of learning. She wrote:

> Interpreting the activity of people without regard for their meaning system and goals renders observations meaningless. We need to understand the coherence of what people from different communities do, rather than simply determining that some other group do not do what 'we' do, or do not do it as well or in the way we do it, or jumping to conclusions that their practices are barbaric. (Rogoff 2003: 17, cited in Larson and Marsh 2005: 101)

Rogoff wants to point to how perspectives that encouraged teacher-led or even student-led classrooms needed to change to consider building communities of practice that reflected the ways humans learn in 'real' circumstances. Cole (1996), following Vygotsky (1978, 1986) had contended that the origins of human thought processes were social. Learning is mutually constituted through a social, cultural and historical process, by interaction with more experienced others both inside and outside the classrooms, utilising the tools available – both physical and intellectual. Rogoff wants to encourage a mutuality of interest and power to exist in classrooms where inhabitants share and build on each other's experiences to construct new knowledge.

The whole idea of 'emergent literacy' (Saracho and Spodek 1993) is based upon the idea that children learn as they are engaged in language activities, both print and oral. Learning to speak, read and write occurs through active participation in social, cultural and historical contexts. As Larson and Marsh (2005: 106) contend:

> In this view, the focus is not on the transferring of literacy knowledge from those who know more to those who know less but on the collaborative use of mediational means, such as literacy, to construct and communicate meaning.

This belief recognises the literacy capabilities that children bring to the classroom from outside. Learning happens through participation.

Cognitive psychological approach

So far, we have stated a view that suggests that learning language is natural to all humans and that we as a species are drawn towards symbolic representation in its different forms – oral and written language, images, dance and music. We have seen that literacy is a social practice learned and utilised within communities to make meaning and knowledge, and that powerful ways of advancing that knowledge are achieved through the making of a community within classrooms that promotes mutuality for all present. Yet, in a great many schools across the advanced, industrialised western world, the practice in classrooms is based upon a completely different perspective. The current advice (and even legislation in some cases) constructs early learners of reading and writing very differently to what we have seen so far.

Both of us have been teachers and academics in England. Here, we have witnessed over the last twelve years the National Literacy Strategy (DfEE 1998), then the Primary National Strategy for Literacy (DfEE 2001). Both documents were hailed by their authors, at the time of their publication, as being the best way to teach literacy and now both have been 'dropped' from government advice. These documents recommended a pedagogy that has its theoretical and ideological foundations in a cognitive psychological (Ehri 1987, 1995) approach (CPA) to learning, and each has left a legacy in *The Simple View of Reading* (DCSF 2009a) which conceives learning as being linear.

Cognitive psychological theory (Ehri 1987, 1995) states that children must be introduced to certain skills and knowledge of literacy at specific ages, as it assumes that all children need to be taught to progress in similar ways. It perceives literacy to be a discrete set of skills that can be learned and taught in a number of different contexts in the same way. This model of literacy has been called *autonomous* (Street 1984). For CPAs, literacy is a neutral package of skills (Street 1995) that can be transferred from one person to another. Street argues that language in this model is treated

> as if it were a 'thing', distanced from both teacher and learner and imposing on them external rules and requirements as though they were passive recipients. (Street and Street 1991: 144)

This is a long way from the community model of learning offered by Rogoff, but is the prevalent model of teaching literacy in developed western societies. It arguably offers instruction at the expense of participation. As Larson and Marsh (2005) point out, these CPAs normalise development through the construction of a neat progression in skills, knowledge and understanding. Children who are unable to acquire these skills at the rate expected are quickly identified as being inadequate in some way and deficit models are established that pathologise children.

The UK's *Independent Review of the Teaching of Early Reading* (Rose 2006), known as the 'Rose Review', makes a case for the systematic teaching of reading by drawing on CPAs. It privileges the teaching of grapho-phonic cueing strategies as the first and most important reading strategy that children must be taught. The Statutory Framework for the Early Years Foundation Stage (EYFS) (DCSF 2007) for children from birth to five years old echoes this 'review' and consolidates Rose's findings by making them statutory. As part of its orders, the EYFS has an educational programme for 'Communication, Language and Literacy' that, out of 19 'Early Learning Goals', has five which relate in some way to the requirement that children learn phonemes – including the stipulation that children must learn to segment and blend them. This legal requirement to teach children phonics at this tender age represents 26 per cent of the total learning goals presented in this section of the document and makes this form of CPA a legal requirement. We would argue it effectively legislates against professionalism and a teacher's professional right to sculpt pedagogy suitable for the children they teach and the contexts within which they practise. A single teaching method that privileges phonics as a reading strategy is now enshrined in law and consequently 'outlaws' alternative approaches.

We need to first contextualise and explain what we mean by 'reading strategies'. From his research and analysis of reading behaviour, Goodman (1967) contended that readers draw on three cueing strategies together to bring meaning from the text: grapho-phonic, syntactic and semantic cues. Grapho-phonic cueing is the way readers are able to decode graphemes (letters) into sounds (phonemes) – blending the phonemes to sound out a word.

Syntactic cueing strategies involve the reader drawing on his/her knowledge of language structures – grammatical constructions. 'The reader using pattern markers such as function words and inflectional suffixes as cues recognises and predicts structures' (Goodman 1973: 25–6). To read well a child must draw on his/her implicit understanding of how spoken language is structured. This enables the child to 'predict' what the next word will be in a written text.

Using semantic cueing strategies, a reader derives meaning from the written word by drawing on their own knowledge about the world and specifically the world within the texts. Knowing that grass can be green and sky can be blue, for example, enables children to predict what the next word will be in a text that has a fine day in the country as a context. A book that depicts the daily goings on in a home kitchen asks the reader to draw on their knowledge of cooking and the general experience of kitchens, utilising the language around this context together. Once again, the reader gives something to the text as well as the text giving something to the reader. With the help of adults and other more experienced readers, children learn to orchestrate their knowledge (Chittenden et al. 2001) about language and the world by drawing on all these cues together. Goodman's approach to cueing strategies reflects his perspectives on honouring and using what children bring to formal learning situations and is in many ways consistent with Rogoff's socio-cultural-historical theories discussed earlier.

CPAs make word identification the most important aspect of reading (Morris et al. 1996). It declares it is more important than other strategies (the semantic and syntactic strategies were thought crucial in the same government's National Literacy Strategy (DfEE 1998) – now 'dumped') and must be taught as the first strategy. Teaching this way, they argue, will lead to better comprehension and readers that are made more efficiently and much faster. One must assume that there is a perception that any kind of community approach would be too indulgent and time-consuming, when children all need to reach specific levels of tested attainment at particular ages to meet government targets.

The prevalent CPA which demands that children are all taught in a precise and consistent linear way is manifested in the current government's document *Letters and Sounds* (DfES 2007) which is a precise strategy for teaching early reading. This claims that the only strategy that should be taught to early readers is phonics. In this document, children are taught in a six-phase (stage) programme for the teaching of phonics throughout Foundation and Key Stage 1. As in all recent policy documentation that offers a precise method of teaching, the authors are always anonymous and this document is no different. The Rose Review which suggests this CPA approach has been heavily criticised by academics and teachers (Hynds 2007; Goouch and Lambirth 2007; Wyse and Styles 2007).

The *Independent Review of the Teaching of Early Reading* (Rose 2006) is clear about how children need to be taught to read from a the youngest age:

> 51. Having considered a wide range of evidence, the review has concluded that the case for systematic phonic work is overwhelming and much strengthened by a synthetic approach. (p. 20)

Synthetic phonics teaches children to convert letters (graphemes) into sounds (phonemes) and then blend the sounds to form recognisable words. The phonemes associated with particular graphemes must each be isolated, pronounced and blended together (synthesised) to read and write the word, for example f/i/g. Children need to be taught from an early age how to segment and blend individual phonemes.

Segmentation means the ability to hear individual phonemes within a word; for instance, the word b/a/sh comprises three phonemes. For the purposes of spelling, a child must be able to segment (or 'sound out') a word into its component phonemes and then choose a letter or combination of letters (e.g. 'sh') to represent each phoneme.

Blending means the ability to merge phonemes together to pronounce a word in its entirety. According to the argument, children will be able to read unfamiliar words phonemically, attributing a phoneme to each letter or letter combination in the word and then merge the phonemes together to pronounce the word.

There is an alternative approach to synthetic phonics called *analytic phonics*. Indeed, for those children who need to be directly taught this way, the two methods should not be seen as incompatible (Hall 2009). However, the Rose Review does not recommend analytical methods. Analytic phonics introduces children to whole words and then teaches them to analyse them into their component parts. This perspective stresses the importance of larger sub-units of words – *onsets* and *rimes* – as well as phonemes (Wyse and Styles 2007). Onset is the part of the syllable before the first vowel. Rime is the part of the syllable from the first vowel onwards: b/un, h/og, t/all, th/ink, s/eat. Analytical phonics methods stress that in English, many single syllable words deviate from the phonetic ideal of using one letter to stand for one vowel, for example the vowel sounds represented by the letter 'a' here: 'cat' , 'car', 'call' and 'cake'.

Analytical phonics methods explain to children that we know how to pronounce the 'a' by looking at the letters that follow it. For example, words ending in 'ar', like 'far' and 'tar' all have the same sound value for the letter 'a', as is the same for the other rimes in the examples we are using here.

The English language is made from an inconsistent orthography, unlike other languages like German that has a consistent orthography (Goswami 2002, 2005), and therefore demands variety and complexity in the methods for teaching it. A single method, as advocated by Rose, is entirely inadequate (Hall 2009).

Analytic and synthetic phonics caused a great many arguments between the two sets of proponents. The National Literacy Strategy's accompanying document was *Progression in Phonics* (DfEE 2000a). This mapped out the stages of phonics teaching that, at the time, government policy-makers deemed to be best. The synthetic phonics advocates (for example, Johnston and Watson 2003) disapproved of the phonics approach that *Progression in Phonics* provided.

These critics pointed to the now famous research completed in Clackmannanshire in Scotland that studied synthetic phonics in a small area of Scotland. This work was hailed by some (Burkard 1999) as 'the Holy Grail of the teaching of reading' and as an end to illiteracy. The work completed in Clackmannanshire stated that synthetic phonics teaching had better results on children's reading achievement than other methods – including analytic phonics.

Yet the Clackmannanshire findings have been criticised for the poor research design and the bias towards synthetic phonics (Goswami 2007). Nonetheless, the media response was to advocate the Clackmannanshire (Johnston and Watson 2005) conclusions. Very quickly afterwards, the Rose Review came out in favour of its use too. However, Rose's findings are highly contested (Wyse and Goswami 2008; Wyse and Styles 2007; Goouch and Lambirth 2007; Hynds 2007). Wyse and Goswami's (2008) rigorous literature review of available research into the efficacy of synthetic phonics states categorically. 'The Rose Report's conclusion that synthetic phonics should be adopted nationally in England is not supported by empirical research evidence' (p. 706). Rose's work has also been accused of political bias. One outspoken critic of Rose states:

> The Rose Review is a cunningly worded, politically motivated, dogmatic and dictatorial document. It purports to be, as witness its title, an 'independent review' of the teaching of early reading, but it's not independent and it is not a review. It is very obviously biased towards one particular 'phonic' method known as 'synthetic phonics' – a method regarded as narrow and limited by most eminent authorities in the field. (Hynds 2007: 271–2)

Conflicting paradigms – conflicting politics

Some of the extremist advocates of a single method CPA for the teaching of early reading take a non-negotiable, didactic response to 'dissent' from their methods. Of course, they now are supported by legislation. The Reading Reform Foundation's website written by Debbie Hepplewhite provides some interesting examples of this form of approach. Hepplewhite writes:

> The degree of subversion and dissent regarding the UK Rose Report amongst established groups such as the unions and the United Kingdom Literacy Association (UKLA) and amongst some local education advisers is astonishing and dismaying. (www.rrf.org.uk/December 2009)

She demands 'vigilance' from parents to observe if schools and teachers dare to stray from this one path. We must presume that the change in the law for the teaching of phonics in the early years presents teachers with the real threat of some form of sanction or punishment. Hepplewhite seems to imply that punishment needs to be applied to those who resist this single method of teaching reading in their schools. As a result, there are real dangers that this kind of control of teachers leads to impoverished practice. Instead of accomplishing the intended methods for rich learning, the teachers' goals are shifted to avoid punishment or to escape 'outing' as a whole language rebel.

We believe the debate about reading and literacy teaching needs to be directed more holistically to what we want our children to meet in their education in terms of teachers, teaching and the learning environment when they enter school classrooms and, as discussed in other chapters, the kinds of readers we want children to become. The models of compliance that extreme advocates of synthetic phonics teaching want our teachers to adhere to in classrooms are totally inappropriate for what we believe education should reflect. Learning to speak, read and write is a cultural process, which needs participation to work alongside a variety of forms of teaching strategies. Teaching needs to be based around what we know about the children in our care, and 'care' needs to be intrinsic to all our interactions with young people in schools. Yet these views, like all those described in this book are linked to their advocates' values and ideology.

What we have described above in terms of CPAs is fundamentally in opposition to pedagogies we advocate in this book. Those outside education have often criticised what seems to be polar differences between the two approaches and the ideological basis of the practice in classrooms. They may be right. Basil Bernstein (2003) established that within the middle-class-controlled education system, principles and values within these controlling factions have produced binaries of approaches and, consequently, serious tensions. Through Bernstein's analytical lens, arguments about how to teach reading take on another dimension.

Policy-makers, educationalists and practitioners have been at loggerheads over conflicting pedagogies which ultimately represent the dynamics of ideas about social control. Bernstein demonstrated that progressive and traditional pedagogies, like those described in this chapter, have their source in particular sections of the middle class. Each section demonstrates a synergy between broader political, economic ideals and aspirations and their approach to education. The section that advocates more traditional approaches, Bernstein argues, is dependent on the economic market, as they are all too often drawn to or have some connection with the economic sector and the entrepreneurial professions. They often will also emphasise vocational education. Progressive pedagogues, on the other hand, are opposed to market forces and favour state-controlled institutions and funding as they are often dependent on them as their source of income. Consequently, they often advocate growth in public expenditure and the expansion of the intervention of the state. They demand that education be removed from vocational considerations (Sadovnik 2001). The so-called 'reading wars' are part of these tensions (Lambirth 2007a). Throughout this chapter, we have argued that one's approach to reading pedagogy is fundamentally linked to the values, ideology and politics of one's vision of the wider society and, as Bernstein would contend, intrinsically part of cultural aspirations and social reproductive trajectories. The answer to the question 'who is right?' will be ideologically rooted in the socio-economic position of those who provide the answer.

Harrison (1999) has argued that where there is no agreement among the research community over an issue, as in this instance over the best ways to teach reading, rhetoric and lobbying become the most effective ways to influence decisions concerning the practice in classrooms. The power to win the support of successive governments and policy-makers over progressive or traditional methods has been relatively interchangeable over recent history. Currently the pendulum has swung in favour of CPAs. We hope to offer an alternative approach in this book, inevitably based on our own values and those of a considerably large group of academics in schools and universities. Our approach will be seen as 'progressive', based upon socio-cultural perspectives and drawing on psycholinguistic insights honed by scholars over the last 40 years.

In this chapter we have introduced readers to some of the important issues and debates surrounding the teaching of early reading and phonics. The authors of this book have 'nailed their colours to the mast' so readers will be fully aware of the research traditions that we follow.

Further reading

Goodman, K. S. (1996) *On Reading*. Portsmouth, NH: Heinemann.

Hynds, J. (2007) 'Putting a spin on reading: the language of the Rose Review', *Journal of Early Childhood Literacy* (special edition, eds K. Goouch, K. Hall, A. Lambirth and P. Shannon), 7(3): 267–81.

3

The role of the teacher

In this chapter we aim:

- to propose that teachers understand the emergence and development of their own literacy and reading practices;
- to show the importance for teachers to understand the nature of reading, in all its forms, structures and guises;
- to emphasise the significance of teachers' knowledge of children, families and communities in their school;
- to describe how research information, theories drawn from experience and statutory responsibilities, all contribute to teachers' professional knowledge.

In the previous chapter we examined very closely the theoretical positions that exist in relation to the teaching of reading and presented research to support our approach. In this chapter we intend to explore the roles played by teachers as children begin to read and progress as readers. We believe teaching to be a complex activity although teaching has been differently defined over generations and is often simply and rather naively used synonymously with instruction. Teaching cannot be seen as an activity in isolation. It needs to be acknowledged that any learning – in this case learning to read – is a process rather than a series of taught events. Learners approach the process from a variety of experiences and with a range of existing knowledge and understanding of the world, and with varying understanding of words, of language and of print. Knowing this, as well as knowing children well and the complexities that are involved in teaching and learning, all contribute to teacher knowledge and inform the roles that teachers employ. We will argue for the knowledge, understanding and subtleties required for the roles involved in teaching reading to be recognised and celebrated, not as 'rocket science' (Rose 2006) but as a professional body of knowledge needed for teaching children to read.

From 1989 onwards, teaching has become increasingly controlled by central government in England and, we would argue, has also as a direct result of this become increasingly instrumental in nature. In the current climate of micro-control over the education of children in schools and early years settings in this country, the philosophy of Durkheim from the early twentieth century would not seem out of place. Durkheim defined education in a not dissimilar way to recent government education initiatives (see, for example, Woodhead 1995; Stannard 1999; Primary Strategy White Paper 2007) claiming the primacy of society over the individual:

> Education is the influence exercised by adult generations on those that are not yet ready for social life. Its object is to arouse and to develop in the child a certain number of physical, intellectual and moral states which are demanded of him by both the political society as a whole and the special milieu for which he is specially destined. (Durkheim, translated and published 1956: 71)

At that point in history children were differently constructed, not as people with rights and responsibilities themselves, with prior experience, aspirations and a sense of self, but as pupils who are to be inducted into a world that is already defined for them: to fit a preordained destiny. In our claims now for a fair and equitable system of education, Durkheim's definition should seem outdated and unjust. However, there is a danger that such principles underpin current teaching policies and practices (the 14–19 Diplomas would be a good example of this) and pervade the roles in which teachers engage in the classroom. In this model, the functions of reading – a functional literacy – would be the goal for teachers. This kind of instrumentalism, defining reading in its most reductionist form as functional in nature, would prompt teachers to reduce their pedagogy to simple and didactic approaches and would assume a causal effect. That is, if children are provided with instruction about a letter sound, then they will learn that letter sound and, further will apply it appropriately in decoding contexts. Of course, this approach, as well as defining reading in its narrowest sense as decoding print, also denies a century of research into teaching and learning, into pedagogy and professional approaches to the teaching of reading. It also denies the work of, for example, Freire (1972) who describes teaching as an act of love, and of other philosophers, pedagogues and researchers who believe that individuals matter in teaching and learning (see, for example, Nutbrown's work on 'respectful relationships' in early education (Nutbrown 1996) and Rinaldi's (2005) definitions of teaching involving a 'pedagogy of relationships').

Teaching is concerned with people: learners who are individuals with dreams and aspirations combined with lived lives, whose experiences are bound up with fantasy and real relationships which compete with imagined and imaginary others; and teachers who have experience of learning, of school and of a lived life, all of which are also culturally bound. Where people are concerned, rather than products, finance, industry or commerce, there are also additional levels of unpredictability, spontaneity, unique responses, imagination, innovation, subversion and interpersonal challenge. In any teaching and learning encounters human factors matter, for example who the teachers and learners are, what experiences and understandings they have in common, a shared language, common relationships, shared knowing.

If, as we believe, teaching and learning centres upon a human encounter (McLean 1991), and is relational in essence (Noddings 1992: 15), then its effectiveness is dependent on the affective nature of the encounter and upon recognition of individuals' knowledge, understanding and experience, motivations and levels of engagement. In many cases it seems that schools have become part of a 'delivery agency model of education' (Young 2006) with more attention given to pre-specified targets and curriculum goals than to children as people – and this is particularly evident in new approaches to the teaching of reading. If such theories are to be challenged then defining the knowledge that teachers need in order to move beyond a delivery model is an important task. Further, it has been claimed that teachers often resort to a narrow didacticism when their own knowledge is weak (David et al. 2000).

Teachers' knowledge

We believe there is no theory-independent way of looking at the world and that teachers cannot claim neutrality. That is, all teachers are people, born into cultures and living in families and communities and with distinct experiences of life and learning that have shaped both the people they are and the teachers they have become. Their plans, their constructions of children, education and learning and their expectations are all set within a cultural frame. In their role as a teacher of reading, their own experiences of learning, of learning to read and of reading themselves will influence their pedagogy at some level. We believe this self-knowledge to be invaluable in helping teachers to appreciate the complexities involved in their own early reading experiences, the range of others involved, the range of texts and the nature of those experiences, whether they believe them now to have been beneficial or not. In understanding their own early reading journey, it is much more likely that teachers will then come to realise that there may be different paths to common outcomes (Clay 1998).

Box 3.1   Teachers should reflect on the following to help them understand themselves as readers and the reading process:

- What are your memories of reading at home?
- Who was influential in helping you?
- What books were involved in your early reading experiences at home?
- Do you remember reading any other types of texts?
- Do you remember favourite places to read?

(Continued)

(Continued)

- Do you have warm memories? If so what are they?
- Do you remember anxiety? If so what was the cause?
- What are your memories of reading at school?
- Do you remember your first teacher reading with you or to you?
- What books do you remember from school?
- Were you encouraged to read any other kinds of texts at school?
- Do you remember reading with anyone else or alone at school?

While this is the first aspect of learning to be acknowledged – and indeed celebrated – there is more to consider in relation to the scope of teachers' knowledge. We believe it to include, at least, the following categories: *knowledge of learning, knowledge of teaching strategies, knowledge of children as learners, knowledge of texts, knowledge of contexts and knowledge of content.* In addition teachers are informed by *research, theory, the practice of others and policy and the politics of education.*

Box 3.2   Teachers need to have a secure bank of knowledge in order to teach reading:

- Knowledge of learning
- Knowledge of children as learners
- Knowledge of teaching strategies
- Knowledge of texts
- Knowledge of contexts
- Knowledge of content
- Knowledge of research
- Knowledge of theories of learning
- Knowledge of the practice of others
- Knowledge of policy
- Knowledge of the politics of education

Teachers' knowledge is demonstrated in the professional narratives they use in their pedagogic lives, which are not always visible or audible to outsiders. For example, teachers' knowledge of children as learners may be demonstrated by the ways in which they interact with children, the voices they employ, the resources they use, the texts they select and the contexts in which the engagement takes place. Some or none of these professional decisions may be explicitly evident in practice or in their engagement with children. Indeed in a busy classroom, it is often difficult for outsiders to deconstruct the practice of the most creative and artistic of teachers without a supporting narration. And so, teachers' knowledge, their professional knowledge, while it may be evidenced in their explicit classroom narratives, is often quite rightly invisible to children and to visiting outsiders who are unused to reading the classroom context.

Nevertheless, such professional knowledge, whether implicit or explicit, is essential for teachers in every aspect of their work, and in this case, in relation to the teaching of reading and phonics.

Knowledge of learning

How children think, develop and learn

In order for teachers to develop empathy for the learners in their care, it is important for them to have gathered information from theory, research and experience of how children see the world and the different ways that children develop physically, emotionally, socially and cognitively. Through such general knowledge teachers are aware of, for example, the stage of physical development of most five-year-old children and so understand their level of fine motor control – for turning the pages of a book or holding a pencil, for the development and control of their mouth and tongue to make sounds, for control of hand/eye coordination, for the amount of time they can be expected to sit still in one position to listen to stories, to read alone, to write. Cognitive development issues include what may be the reasonable expectations that can be made of children of a particular age, for example, to follow instructions, to visually and aurally remember letters and sounds, to reproduce them, to hold meaning in their memory, to make connections with other experiences, to make connections between existing knowledge and new information. Such knowledge will help teachers not only to plan generally a range of potential learning experiences for the children of that age but also to identify variances in their class and to replan according to the needs of individual children who may not fit the expected pattern of learning. In turn, close observations will serve to further teacher knowledge and add to their repertoire of learning experiences. In this way, although teachers know that classes of children always vary from one year to the next, they are able to make professional judgements about reasonable expectations of children at each stage in the knowledge that all children are different and may have had vastly different early experiences of literacy and of life.

Box 3.3

- What do you know about children's early learning?
- What do you understand about early literacy learning?
- What early encounters may help children to read?
- What do children need to know in order to choose to read?

(Continued)

(Continued)

- How do children need to have developed physically in order to handle a book?
- What do you know about children's cognitive development in relation to learning to read?
- What kinds of experiences do you believe will enrich children's early literacy learning?

Acknowledgement of prior experiences

Information about the experiences that children will have encountered before school may not be easy to access in any accurate form and it would be problematic to make assumptions about children's prior literacy experiences based on scant knowledge. The first rule here, however, is you can be sure that in general no two children will have had the same experiences and a whole class certainly cannot be assumed to have had the same prior experiences of literacy. Secondly, even the child's first teacher can be confident that the child will have experienced literacy in one form or another before or outside of the school context. This may not take the form of traditional school literacy (see, for example, the seminal work of Brice Heath 1983) and may consist mostly, for example, of screen literacy of one sort or another, comic-based experiences or oral literacy. It is important to acknowledge and celebrate these experiences and build new connections from them, but it is also important to remember that all children inhabit the same print-filled world, where homes, shops, streets, television screens, computers and hand-held technology all confront children with print from a very early age. Babies are born with a predisposition for curiosity and children grow to develop a 'ravenous appetite for meaning making' (Kress 1997: 33). And so bridges must be built between the print environment in which children live, grow and learn to mean and new literacies introduced in school, in order to help children make sense of each encounter.

Box 3.4   What do you feel you need to find out about a child's early experiences?

- Early experiences with books and stories
- Early experiences with other texts
- Attitude to books
- Establishment of favourites
- Ability to select from a range
- Ability to listen to stories
- Interest in print, in pictures

- Interest in re-reading
- Noticing print in different contexts, e.g. in supermarkets
- Recognising letters from name
- Recognition of whole words in context
- Interest in print generally in environment
- Interest in writing
- Holding pens/pencils with ease
- Ability to write initial letter of name/whole name
- Mark making
- Making signs or notices
- Writing letters
- Covering pages in marks
- Copying letters
- Making lists

Connections to home cultures, home learning, outside school contexts

It is perhaps difficult for teachers either to know about or to appreciate and celebrate the range of cultures among which the children in their care have already learned to live. However, by prioritising this knowledge and demonstrating respect for cultural difference, through literacy children can be helped to make positive connections between home and school cultures and home and school literacy. This may be partly achieved through the books and stories represented in the class, although it has been found that children themselves are quite adept at mixing together literacy practices from a range of sources, resulting in 'syncretic literacy', a term created through research carried out with Bangladeshi-British children and families in London (Gregory and Williams 2000). Although national policy often refers to home/school reading contracts and schools frequently require parents to commit to reading from prescribed reading books with their children at home, it seems that many children are involved in much more complex and self-motivating literacy practices out of school than has previously been acknowledged. While some of the literacy activities in children's homes in Gregory and Williams' research centred upon traditional school texts, others were part of 'unofficial literacies' (Gregory and Williams 2004: 34) in both western and non-western homes which ranged across a number of contexts, including learning about reading from horse racing tips in the newspaper, playing computer games with siblings and participating in Bengali classes. One of the key elements in children's home literacy practice seemed to be the existence of 'literacy brokers', that is a parent, grandparent or older sibling who would attend to, mediate, scaffold, tutor or listen to a child reading. Any assumption that children come to school 'clean', without literacy, would be mistaken. The challenge is to find ways in which children can be supported in drawing together the unofficial literacies of home with the official school literacy that is required of them.

Box 3.5   Find out about the school's locality:

- Ask about ethnic schooling in the area.
- Talk to children about outside literacy practices.
- Ask parents about outside literacy practices.
- Try to establish links with local community groups.
- Find out if its possible to observe in a local ethnic school (often Saturday mornings).
- Look for ethnic/cultural associations and websites.
- Find out more about languages, religion and religious practices.
- Invite parents and other community members into school to read with children.
- Invite parents and others to translate favourite picture book texts into other local languages.

In a way then the teacher becomes the 'professional literacy broker', drawing on and learning from early practices and selecting and connecting with new opportunities.

Knowledge of teaching strategies

As teachers develop clear knowledge of children as literacy learners, who are thinking, developing and learning at different paces and in different ways, both inside and outside of school and among different cultural experiences, they will also learn of the need to develop a repertoire of teaching strategies to support the range of learners that children comprise. These strategies are professionally crafted and often subtly applied and contained within the vast depths of teachers' Mary Poppins-like carpet bag of skills, strategies and roles. Instruction – with the whole class, small groups, pairs or individual children – is but one of the strategies available to teachers who will also know of a range of other ways to help children to read.

We believe that, in order to teach children to read, the teacher first has to ensure a close engagement with the learners, with the learners' experiences and with the texts that matter to them. We reject any notion that children can be taught to read in a dispassionate manner. Teachers of reading need to demonstrate their interest in children as readers, their interest in children's reading habits and their interest in texts, print books and stories.

With their knowledge of the different ways that children learn, teachers will employ a range of multi-sensory approaches to enable them to access print texts. Shared reading opportunities have traditionally been employed in early years settings to induct children into reading books and now this strategy has been successfully used throughout primary, and indeed can occasionally be found in the early stages of Key Stage 3. In this way, through sharing together a text that children could not easily access alone, developing readers are able to both hear and see print being coded into sound – the grapheme/phoneme relationship – and experience the ways that teachers as expert readers access print. In these kinds of contexts teachers will model the way they can 'do the voices' of story and engage with humour in children's literature as well as demonstrate the ways that information texts can be used and the different reading strategies that may need to be employed. The two strategies of guided reading and guided writing are also both essential in providing opportunities for children and their teachers to encounter print together as they construct and write print (encode), deconstruct and read print (decode) and articulate and read print aloud (recode) – all key constituent features of a reading class-room. When teachers delve into their vast carpet bag of skills and knowledge to plan and engage in shared and guided reading activities they will:

- offer high levels of support, drawing children into texts and ensuring all have access;
- use the opportunity to maximise connections with children's prior experiences and existing knowledge;
- differentiate shared and guided activities to extend the children's levels of understanding;
- identify features of print;
- focus on known areas of development relating to phonics, syntax and semantic elements;
- instruct children in relation to phonics;
- use multi-sensory approaches;
- model ways of reading print;
- engage with the humour in children's texts;
- create intertextual links;
- make connections between children's emerging skills as writers and the print in shared texts;
- create activities in which children can collaborate to read and to write;
- introduce additional resources and prompts to help children to read a text;
- alert children's attention to environmental print to help them make connec-tions with other reading;
- provide a wealth of reasons for children to talk about print (about which more in a later chapter) and gossip about texts.

As can be seen from the above, 'instruction' is simply one tool that can be found in the carpet bag of tools available to teachers. While it may be impor-tant, it is not sufficient on its own. As teachers develop secure and informed knowledge about how children develop as learners and as readers, the peda-gogy of reading employed will become embedded within a strong and confi-dent early years/primary pedagogy centred on supporting and developing children's early predispositions to be curious and to learn. This knowledge, coupled with children's early natural desire to draw adults into their learning worlds, will ensure a close engagement with each child's developing skills and abilities.

Knowledge of children as learners

Knowing children appears to be a straightforward idea and it will be assumed that all teachers know the children in their care. However, the ways in which the current system of schooling and assessment of learning operates does not necessarily require individuals to be 'known' and children in schools are often referred to by levels, sets or ability groups rather than by name. Already it can be seen that teaching children to read is complex and learning to read cannot be separated from learning other skills, developing other attitudes and capitalising on other resources. For children at the early stages of developing competence in reading, that is children from the early years of education through primary stages, making connections with other aspects of their learning and their lives is important. This is why the learning of 'contextualised' print is more successful than the short-term gains of learning isolated sounds. The development of intentional learners who are keen to pursue their interests through print texts, as well as other sources, and are adept in making and learning from analogous connections in relation to print must be a key aim of teachers at this stage. This is why it is so important to know individual children well in order to support them to be persistent and voracious in their searches for meaning through print. Such knowledge includes the following:

- *Knowledge of the complexities involved in children's learning* – that is, knowing children well enough to help them in making connections with other aspects of their learning and their lives;
- *Knowledge of the context, communities and cultural backgrounds of children* – in order to help children to make sense of the information they are gathering about reading both inside and outside of school contexts and to use information drawn from all sources;
- *Knowledge of the impact of other children on individuals' learning* – using collaborative activities where appropriate to meet children's needs but being aware of the dynamics involved in groups and the sensitive growth of children's self-esteem;
- *Knowledge of children in relation to their families* – to help children and their families to seek guidance where appropriate and to provide additional support and resources where children seem to need it; also to draw children's families where possible into the reading community of the school.

Knowledge of texts

Teachers' professional knowledge has traditionally been bound up with their knowledge of texts used in teaching and learning. Today, in the twenty-first century, this has become a huge task as the publication of books for children has become such a broad, international, multi-million pound, economic concern. However, to have a working knowledge of books published for children is an essential professional ingredient and to have an intimate knowledge of a large repertoire of books is an absolutely crucial feature of teaching children to read and teaching children about reading at all stages of education. It is also important to model knowledge of books to children to allow them to see how essential it is to be a member of the reading club (Smith 1985). This we believe should not be an elite group but have an open membership across social class, gender and race. This is becoming an important debate in England as policy appears to be moving towards grading the kinds of books available to children in school at different stages, with 'simply decodable books' in danger of becoming the reading diet for the youngest children in school before graduating to books, stories and information texts written by authors for the real purpose of engaging readers in their content rather than the phoneme count of included words. We believe that teachers who are readers themselves, who have a deep knowledge of what books are good for, will not entertain 'simply decodable books' in their classroom if they seem purposeless. Projects that have engaged teachers in developing their own literacy practice in order to be better positioned to support children's development have been particularly successful (Cremin et al. 2008).

Historically, books were written almost anonymously, with little known about their authors or their origins. Now, children's authors and illustrators have become part of the hugely developing commercial world of children's publishing. Teachers' knowledge of authors is important in directing children towards appropriate texts, next steps and more works by the same author. It is also important to help children to develop their knowledge of how print comes into existence in books and the key relationship between reading and writing. As children learn that books are indeed written by a person, with their own interests and passions, so too will children see the possibility of authoring their own texts.

While children are encountering a range of texts outside school contexts, in schools we are focusing our attention mainly (and some may say mistakenly in this age of multiple literacies) on print texts, mostly books. There is some evidence to say that children are busy in their homes and outside environments collecting information about print in purposeful contexts. The letters that begin and are included in their names become enormously important to children and are frequently the letters they use in their early and emerging encounters with writing, using these repeatedly metaphorically or in a sign-holding way (see, for example, Kress 1997) when writing messages, notices or recounts. The seminal work of Marie Clay is useful in understanding these early print awareness stages. In addition, children are making sense of print when it is embedded in visual texts and on computer screens and hand-held games. Although we acknowledge the continuing high status of print texts in contemporary society, we are also keenly aware of the messages that children are receiving from their own worlds about the place of print among other forms of literacy. It is undoubtedly important for teachers to acknowledge with children in their practice that print literature is but one form of text at use in society, although of high status.

Knowledge of contexts

Teachers' knowledge of the contexts in which children live and grow as readers is important in their quest to serve children well in their reading development. This knowledge is of importance in two ways. First, it will empower teachers to draw on, for example, popular culture texts to make connections for children in their learning. In this way, teachers can embed activities to support children's developing alphabetic knowledge, phonemic knowledge and phonological knowledge in a context that will be of interest to children and will help to motivate them in school contexts. Second, it provides teachers with additional knowledge about the sources and messages informing children about literacy generally and print literacy in particular in order that they may capitalise on these or counter them. Socially, for example, children may be using text messaging or social networking sites that use different forms of printed text to convey meaning and these quickly achieve high value in children's lives, even those of quite young children. While not wishing to devalue these in social contexts, it is important for teachers to be aware of their influence and to help children to be aware of the differences between these and more conventional uses of print text. As previously mentioned, Gregory and Williams (2000) give examples of how children have learned to read from a grandfather who is interested in racing tips in the newspaper and others who are learning to read in out-of-school Bengali classes. Knowledge of the learning in which children are engaged in other contexts is of great use to teachers as they build on and extend children's print repertoires in school.

Box 3.6

- Ask the children in the class about the technology they use at home.
- Do they own an ipod, a lap-top, hand held devices?
- Which video games do they enjoy?
- Which websites do they use?
- Do they use technology at home on their own or with others?
- Are they limited in the amount of use of these devices?

Knowledge of content

In this chapter we are aware that describing the role of teachers and the levels and range of knowledge required of teachers could be all consuming. We are clear, however, that without this knowledge, simple phonics instruction will be insufficient to help children to read. However, the Department for Children, Schools and Families makes very clear its special emphasis on phonics as it has now established a new Phonics website, listing products, publishers and associated links within the Standards site. To ensure the message is transmitted to teachers, changes are included in the Primary Literacy Framework (DCSF 2007), the Early Years Foundation Stage (DCSF 2007) in their National Training Programme in Communication Language and Literacy and in their own resource for phonics training *Letters and Sounds* (Primary National Strategy 2007). The two key changes are in the early years where 'a systematic phonic approach' is reflected in an Early Learning Goal; the other is in the English programme of study at Key Stage 1 which requires children to 'employ their phonic knowledge as their first strategy in reading' (DCSF 2007). Recommendations from the Rose Review (2006) have now been absorbed into government discourse. However, the Early Years Framework, which is the statutory requirement for providers in the Early Years Foundation Stage as discussed in Chapter 2, makes clear in the statement about principles for learning and development that 'children develop and learn in different ways and at different rates' and highlights the interconnections across areas of learning for children, stressing the importance of people, enjoyment, a range of resources and the importance of rhyme, rhythm and alliteration in developing links between sounds and letters. In addition, Rose (2006) acknowledged the importance of teachers using their *professional judgement* in addressing children's needs in relation to reading development and appropriate stages for instruction, and this has been reiterated on the DCSF Standards site (www.standards.dcsf.gov.uk) and in other national government documents. In order to do so, however, teachers need to be clear about the politics and policy context within which the content of national frameworks and curricula are constructed.

The complex nature of the teaching of reading

This chapter has claimed that the focus of teachers' roles in relation to teaching reading is to ensure that they are knowledgeable. Set out above are the complex and wide-ranging areas of knowledge that we claim are required to be effective. We believe that the skills, abilities, attitudes and attributes needed by teachers are embedded within this knowledge set. In addition, however, there are some key elements that will contribute to children's ability to acquire and employ alphabetic and phonemic knowledge as well as their ability to use other information to both decode and to read in functional, purposeful and enjoyable ways. In an academically rigorous and widely celebrated research report, findings indicating the effectiveness of some teachers included the following:

- The effective teachers of literacy had an extensive knowledge of the content of literacy.
- Because of this knowledge they were able to see, and help their pupils to see, connections between the text, sentence and word levels of language.

- The effective teachers had coherent belief systems about literacy and its teaching and these were generally consistent with the ways they chose to teach.
- These belief systems, and hence teachers' teaching practices, tended to emphasise the importance of children being clear about the purposes of reading and writing and of using this clarity of purpose as a means of embedding the teaching of grammar, phonics, etc. into contexts which made sense to the children.
- The ways (and the possibility) that children have already encountered sounds, letter sounds and letter names prior to and outside of school.
- The range of information that children will need to draw upon in order to read.

(Medwell et al. 1998: 81)

In spite of convincing research evidence such as the above, in England as well as in the United States we are working in our classrooms with 'government imposition of intensive, direct phonics instruction' (Strauss and Altwerger (2007: 316). Even those most closely associated with the intended outcomes of current government dictats in relation to phonics and the teaching of reading argue against the 'top-down managerial way ... When you have someone who tells you exactly what to do, you tend to follow it in a mechanical manner ... it is not being done with any real conviction' (Burkard, cited in Scott 2010: 2). In the study quoted above, the belief systems of the teachers were felt to have contributed to the success of their teaching.

Finally, there are some absolute essentials in relation to the role of teachers in teaching reading and in teaching decoding skills – a small but significant aspect of learning to read – and they include the following:

Provision

It is the teacher's role to provide:

- a brilliantly rich, and print-rich, environment;
- the best resources possible and facilitate their use;
- the best books there are available;
- opportunities to read, often and at least every day;
- reasons for reading;
- space in which reading can occur comfortably.

Planning

It is the teacher's role to plan:

- a rich, interactive and sometimes playful literacy pedagogy;
- a combination of direct instruction and completely independent reading times;
- to read to children as frequently as possible, but at least once a day;
- opportunities for children to read to and with each other;
- to assess and to understand children's development and progress as readers.

Conclusion

We began this chapter by establishing the absolute need for teachers to be knowledgeable. We have carefully defined the nature of such knowledge and described ways in which teachers can enhance their understanding of children, of their environments, of their prior experience and of their knowledge of reading before and outside of school. We have asked teachers to examine their own literacy and particularly their reading histories to support their understanding of the emergence of literacy skills. In addition, we have identified the kind of information that teachers need to seek from families and communities to help them to know children as readers. Finally we have drawn the chapter together by attempting to summarise the teacher's role. With the benefit of this extensive range of knowledge, and with the understanding that such knowledge will help them to relate closely to the young learners in their care and their development and learning needs, teachers are in the best possible position to plan appropriate ways to enrich and progress children's reading.

Further reading

Kress, G. (1997) *Before Writing: Rethinking the Paths to Literacy.* Abingdon: Routledge.
Medwell, J., Wray, D., Poulson, L. and Fox, R. (1998) *Effective Teachers of Literacy.* Exeter: Exeter University.

4

Knowledge for reading

In this chapter we aim:

- to demonstrate that all children need to read beyond a functional level;
- to describe reading as more than decoding;
- to propose that the knowledge required for reading is wide-ranging and includes knowledge of the alphabet, knowledge of the sounds and patterns in language (phonological knowledge), knowledge of the joy to be found in books and stories, including books to inform, knowledge of and about language. We believe that knowledge about books and authors is central to all other knowledge about reading.

What kind of reader do we want to produce, and for what and whose ends? (Kress 1997: 47)

The question above is crucial and needs to be considered seriously. The assumption in the question is that there is more than one kind of reader. In this chapter we will argue that there are possibly two kinds of reader – the first is a functional reader, that is someone who can decode print and make sounds that match the marks on the page, blend them together and pronounce a word – recoding print into sound (Goswami 2007). The second kind of reader knows that there is more to reading (and writing) than simply decoding and recoding print. We would argue that everyone needs to be sufficiently competent in reading to make us 'unworried by the notices at the bus stop' (Meek 1982: 17), that is to feel at ease in what has become a world completely dominated by print. However, we would also argue with Meek that there is more to reading than this. To be a full participant in our contemporary world we must not only be able to read but also be able to ask questions about the print we encounter, to challenge the written word, to investigate it, explore its meanings, recognise its subtleties and to read the unwritten – the meaning behind words. This kind of reading, 'beyond a utilitarian view of literacy' (Meek 1982: 18) is the ultimate goal for teachers and demands that readers read for their own purposes. In answer to Kress, we believe that these are the kinds of readers that we want to help to produce.

Some claim that this kind of reading should follow on from acquiring the ability to simply decode (see Gough and Tunmer's 'Simple View of Reading', in Rose 2006: 78) and that this enriched reading experience can only be possible once children learn that letters stand for sounds. Theoretically, of course, this approach does sound sensible. However, we know from research and from practice that this simply will not do. Even in theory simple phonic instruction, synthetic phonics now prescribed by government, will not work as we know that the English language, unlike other language systems, is irregular (see Strauss and Altwerger 2007; Goswami 2007) and that simple phonic instruction will only provide limited information that may serve to mislead beginning readers and cause disaffection. Politicians often argue for the 'common-sense' approach to teaching reading and promote the obviously inaccurate view that phonics is a simple solution which involves the pretence that the letters in the alphabet only make one sound (Rosen 2006).

Listen to Goswami's description of 'symbol systems (orthographies)':

> Most Western European languages use an alphabetic orthography. Languages like Korean, Hindi, Chinese and Japanese do not. For example, Chinese and Japanese use character-based scripts. All these types of visual symbol share one core feature. They can be recoded into sound. Teaching children 'phonics' provides direct instruction in how to achieve this recoding to sound. Phonics instruction teaches children how the visual symbol system of their language represents the sounds of the words in their language. (Goswami 2007: 124)

This description puts phonics instruction clearly in its place – as a method of recoding symbols into sound. Phonics instruction does not teach children to read. We know that reading involves significantly more than knowing the sound/symbol relationship. Studies of children who are competent readers have shown that most find that dependence on phonic knowledge is insufficient and that 'the blending of sound segments was simply not a workable strategy' (Barrs and Meek Spencer 2007: 151). In fact there is a complex web of knowledge that is required and this needs to be 'orchestrated' by the reader in order to both 'recode' text and to read with fluency and meaning,

Children learn to read when they are affectively engaged, when they want to read, when it matters to them to do so. Simple instruction in alphabetic and phonemic principles will not create *readers* of either kind. It will create children who can chant and recite alphabetic and phonemic information. We maintain that the two kinds of reading experience are both important but that they must work together and that children will attend to print when they are intrinsically motivated to be involved in literacy activities.

Knowledge for reading

What is it then that children need to know to become fluent and enthusiastic readers, to be motivated to read, and, as a consequence of this information, what do teachers need to provide and to do in order to ensure that children read? Teachers live in a rather confusing world. Their work is controlled and effectively monitored by central government (Hall 2004; Goouch and Lambirth 2007); their pedagogy is determined for them; policy documents are delivered frequently; government websites provide free downloadable material; commercial companies inundate them with advertising; everybody they encounter is an expert on the teaching of reading – and messages often conflict (Alexander 2010; Whitehead 2009). In subsequent chapters very clear information will be given about how we believe children can be taught to read. We will use examples from practice to illustrate our ideas and demonstrate how best children can be helped to read. To begin, and following the introductory chapters relating to the political and policy context and the role of the teacher, it is important to establish what knowledge for the kinds of reading described above might mean and from where this might be gained. This will then lead to suggestions about the type of pedagogy to employ and the environment to create.

Knowledge for reading is complex and so will be divided into the following sections: *alphabetic knowledge, knowledge of the pleasure of reading and what reading is good for, Knowledge of how books work, vocabulary knowledge and knowledge about language, and knowledge of texts and authors.* This list is not arranged hierarchically, nor is it exclusive – teachers may be able to add to it themselves. We have, however, begun with alphabetic knowledge simply because this is the area that most readers of this book may be most familiar with and may need to be reassured about.

Alphabetic knowledge

We are keenly aware that, as the sounds in our language can be represented by symbols, the acquisition of this kind of knowledge is important. These 'small shapes' are already a part of children's lives before they come to school and most children have become familiar with the shape of their own name and other familiar symbols in and around their homes. Building on and extending this knowledge is the next step for these developing readers and this can only be achieved through gaining some understanding of what children already know and then planning experiences to further this knowledge.

Developing children's alphabetic knowledge is best achieved by using the same pedagogy appropriate for any other aspect of young children's education, that is, through play, exploration, rehearsal and shared and supported activities. Above all, children need to see the sense in what they are doing and they need to see how this learning can be of use to them. This can be achieved through playing games with letters and sounds but also by embedding this kind of knowledge transmission in activities involving connected text. Traditionally, in early years classrooms, shared reading and shared writing have been core ways of talking about print with children within contexts carrying meaning. Children's attention can be drawn to familiar letters, letter strings, patterns and rhymes, onsets and rimes of words while the story or book focus is still maintained. Very young children who have been read to from an early age are quite used to identifying letters from their own name in printed text, to matching familiar or repeated words, to turning pages back to find the same sounding word and so on. Embedding alphabetic instruction in shared texts is simply an extension of this kind of intimate book-sharing activity that may have already occurred. Of course for those children who have not yet experienced being read to at home, including these book-sharing, print-awareness activities in a non-threatening environment at school becomes even more essential.

Box 4.1   Letter knowledge:

- Establishing the need for displays, authentic labels and notices to be made by children
- The provision of physical materials to explore and play with, for example sand, paint, dough, 'gloop' to make letter shapes
- Shared reading with high-quality alphabet books
- Reciting alphabet rhymes/songs frequently
- Lining up for lunch, etc. in alphabetic order of names
- Playing games:

  - Hangman
  - Snap with made cards
  - I spy

- Playing round-the-class games like:

  - My cat is clever, cute, cuddly ...
  - I went to the shop and bought an apple, a banana, a cake ...

- Accessing software – there is now a range of animated alphabets to be found
- Creating alphabets that are personal to the class, for example name alphabets, favourite food alphabets, 'we like ...' alphabets – these can be in the form of friezes or books
- Making cooked dough letters
- Creating letter searches in comics, magazines or newspapers; using a seconds timer and giving the children highlighter pens to find, for example, 20 lower case letters of their name initial in 20 seconds ...

Phonological knowledge

Alphabet knowledge does not end with letter knowledge. Children also need to become familiar with the patterns and sounds in language. This has of course already begun before children start school and, for many children, from birth as in families a wealth of nursery rhyme knowledge is often passed down. Knowledge of traditional nursery rhymes is not the only source of phonological understanding, however. Families are often a rich source of poetry, rhyme and song. And while the whole of a poem may not be remembered or recited in families, 'he has opened all his parcels but the largest and the last ...' may be part of birthday present opening rituals; 'faster than fairies, faster than witches, bridges and houses, hedges and ditches' – may accompany train journeys, or 'diddle, diddle dumpling' might be heard when pyjamas are being put on. More likely now though is that children will have a rhythmic backcloth of advertisement jingles or songs from *X Factor*. Whatever we think of the cultural benefits of either range, both will provide children with information about how our language works and the repetition, predictable rhymes, patterns and refrains will provide a structure on which children learn to depend. Filling in the end rhyme, for example 'Humpty Dumpty sat on the wall, 'Humpty Dumpty had a great ...', is a common feature of home practices and will help children to become sensitive to rhyme and rhythm. Drawing on development at home, classrooms will need to have a supply of picture books with patterned and predictable language to use during shared reading as well as anthologies of poetry and nursery rhymes.

> 'Barrs and Ellis are arguing here for good quality stories written by authors whose main concern is to entertain and delight young children, while at the same time supporting them in developing a familiarity with print'

Such books will quickly become familiar to children and will be the kinds of books that children will want to come back to, will find comfort in and, as developing readers, will feel safe in their company. Making books of favourite nursery rhymes, favourite song lyrics and favourite advert jingles will all help children to see how the sounds that they hear can also be written. Drawing together these three strands in this kind of activity – of hearing language, writing it down and reading – will help children to see their interconnectedness and to learn about the structures of language and story in the safety of frequently revisited texts. Children soon learn to tune into the sounds of language and of storybook language and begin to appropriate it for themselves.

Box 4.2   Books to support phonological understanding:

- *We're Going on a Bear Hunt* (Michael Rosen/Helen Oxenbury)
- *Not Now, Bernard* (David McKee)
- *Each Peach Pear Plum* (Janet and Allan Ahlberg)
- *Brown Bear, Brown Bear* (Bill Martin/Eric Carle)
- *Cat on the Mat* (Brian Wildsmith)
- *How Do I Put It On?* (Shigeo Watanabe)
- *Where's My Teddy?* (Jez Alborough)
- *All Join In* (Quentin Blake)
- *On the Way Home* (Jill Murphy)
- *Once Upon a Time* (John Prater)
- *The House that Jack Built* (Colin and Jacqui Hawkins)
- *Don't Forget the Bacon* (Pat Hutchins)
- *This Is the Bear* (Sarah Hayes/Helen Craig)
- *Room on the Broom* (Julia Donaldson/Axel Scheffler)
- *Dear Zoo* (Rod Campbell)
- *The Kingfisher Playtime Treasury* (Pie Corbett/Moira and Colin Maclean)

Knowledge of the pleasure of reading and what reading is good for

> Pleasure and empowerment are not literacy 'add-ons' which come as optional extras when the struggles with words are over; they are the essential foundations and the rationale for learning to be literate. (Whitehead 1999: 53)

There is clear evidence from international research (Progress in International Reading Study (PIRLS): Mullins 2006; Programme for International Student Assessment (PISA): OECD 2009) that children in England are not yet scoring highly in relation to children in other countries, with enjoyment of reading, or reading for pleasure, significantly lower among children in this country who also are reported as having less confidence in reading. As well as being able to read for functional reasons, there are clear benefits from affectively engaging in reading. Research reports suggest, perhaps unsurprisingly, that 'reading for pleasure is seen to be positively correlated with positive attitudes to reading' (Cremin 2007: 167).

Most, but not all, children learn about the pleasurable nature of texts and contexts for stories long before they start school and continue with this outside of school. Bedtime stories, songs, language play and games are an integral part of some families' lives. Early induction into literacy in affective and engaging events provides children with positive reading lessons before they are able to recognise alphabet symbols or realise the significance of print. In these early lessons children are learning to enjoy reading and story and beginning to appreciate the connection with their emotional lives, with how they think and feel and, importantly, the connection with how others live. In this way children develop as readers who 'are at home in the life of the mind; [who] live with ideas, as well as events and fact' (Meek 1982: 17). In addition, children learn that literacy can be engaging for other reasons, when it involves reading and writing party invitations for example, purposeful when writing signs and notices like 'keep out' signs for bedroom doors, and companionable when comics, stories, catalogues, etc. can be shared with friends and family.

There is an enormous responsibility then for school to continue with these themes, to introduce them to children who have not been privileged to share books and stories at home, while at the same time extending, enriching and monitoring children's reading. Demonstrating the pleasure to be gained from reading is an important part of shared reading experiences and that requires teachers to know books well in order to be able to share their enthusiasm. As Meek says, 'we only read well what we think well of' (Meek 1982: 45) and so a deep immersion into the world of children's literature is essential for teachers if they are to arouse enthusiasm and model positive reading behaviours. In order to teach reading, teachers must become readers.

Modelling and developing positive attitudes to reading is a key focus in teaching reading. Once children become aware of what can be gained in terms of pleasure and purpose, then not only will they become self-motivated to engage in reading but good reading habits will be formed.

Box 4.3   Help children to experience pleasure in reading and to know what can be gained from reading by:

- Reading books, stories and poems aloud, frequently but at least once a day.
- Allowing or even positively encouraging children to re-read favourite stories.
- Providing time for children to talk about books and stories and other texts in their lives, as well as school texts.
- Introducing children to a range of texts on areas of interest to *them*, which will include information books, information on the internet, other screen texts, stories, poetry …
- Creating opportunities for children to engage in book gossip.
- Talking about books you have read, perhaps reading extracts from your own reading.
- Celebrating children's favourite texts through re-tellings, displays, etc.
- Using Chambers' 3 sharings model – sharing enthusiasms, sharing puzzles, sharing connections. (Chambers 1993: 16)

Chambers talks about changing children from being 'flat-earth' readers into 'not just round-earth but intergalactic readers' (1993: 13) and claims that the key from his surveys of adult readers is that:

As children we had all been affected, and still were, by what others whom we liked, respected and would listen to, said about books they had read, and which we then read because of their encouragement. And we had all been affected, and still were, by what we found ourselves saying during everyday conversation about what we'd read. (Chambers 1993: 14)

If children are allowed to see how pleasurable reading can be, if a classroom ethos can be created that 'fuels delight and fosters desire' (Cremin 2007: 185), then there is no reason why children cannot find their own and other worlds in reading.

Knowledge of how books work

Traditionally, teachers of reading, including parents, have been content to instruct children about the fact that print moves from left to right and from the top of the page to the bottom, in the conventions of English language, and that books generally start from the beginning, the first page, and journey towards the end, the last page. This has to be seriously revised now, first, because the texts that children encounter are wide-ranging and complex. They may be found on screens as frequently as inside the covers of a book. And second, there is the fact that authors and illustrators of all texts are much more creative in their use of 'the page' now and print is often to be found dancing around the edges of illustrations, in speech bubbles, under flaps, travelling across two pages, moving around the edge of a page, travelling diagonally across a page and so on. But children have become used to that as their worlds are made up of rapidly moving images, animated texts and interactive print on screens. In many ways, children are in a better position to work out how texts and books work now as there are so many different versions freely available to them as they grow up in fast-moving visual worlds. Children will also have found in some of their early encounters with books that there may be games to be played and explorations to be enjoyed as well as complex illustrations to be pored over. While there are many excellent straightforward print texts available to children, there are also musical books, textured books, stories with hidden characters, books with holes in the pages through which characters disappear (in Lauren Child's work, for example), books that have beginnings at the front and then from the back (for example Anthony Browne's *The Tunnel*) and so on. These kinds of books require readers to take ownership of the reading experience, to play the games designed for them or simply to enjoy the stories. In his examination of new literacies and how the faces of texts have changed over time, Kress has identified how print and image have changed places during the last several decades with image now taking a major role and print much less so. In both story and information books this is evident, perhaps lessening the traditional distance between the two. Picture books for children are celebrated as having the right combination of ingredients to draw children into reading:

> Pictures and words together telling a story – it is a magical combination. It is a combination that accounts for the popularity of films, theatre, television drama, pantomime, Punch and Judy, opera, comics, graphic novels and I'm sure much else. The picture book is unforgettable mental nourishment, furnishing us with images and tunes for life. (Graham 2004: 1)

Exploring the world of picture books, finding that each may have a unique way of telling a story, provides children with special kinds of knowledge: knowledge that games can be played with pictures and words; knowledge that pictures can tell stories with and without the support of words; knowledge that you, as the reader, have to do varying amounts of work to construct meaning from the text; knowledge that sometimes texts are unpredictable; and knowledge of probably much more. And once acquired, this knowledge will always be of use to them in their development as readers and writers.

Box 4.4

- Ensure children have access to a full range of books that work differently – including *The Tunnel; This is the Book that Jack Made* ...
- Provide time for children to interrogate texts and pictures.
- Demonstrate reading complex texts for children during shared reading times.
- Provide time and opportunities for children to share and explore books with friends.
- Read information books to children as well as stories.
- Read complex texts alongside individual children, pairs or small groups.
- Tell children the vocabulary of books and define terms for them, for example:

  - character
  - plot
  - setting
  - illustration
  - dedication/acknowledgements
  - blurb
  - publisher
  - author
  - illustrator
  - play script
  - information text
  - fiction/non-fiction
  - contents
  - index.

- Make books with and for children.
- Create groups of children for the production of books, i.e. an author, illustrator, publisher ...
- Include children's own books in the book corner.

Vocabulary knowledge and knowledge about language

We have already talked about the ways that children first encounter language, that is within family and in home contexts, in familiar environments and in the company of familiar and literate 'others'. We know that children grow up in worlds in which they are surrounded by print in meaningful contexts. In this way young children learn valuable lessons about language. They first learn that it matters; they learn that both spoken and written language make a difference to the ways that people behave and respond. Very sophisticated learning occurs as children begin to grasp the nature and use of spoken language and they achieve this without direct instruction. In young children's worlds, objects are given labels and important objects are quickly named by children. They learn the labels for important people, *mum, dad, grannie*, etc. and for important things, *dinner, milk, bottle, teddy* for example, and possessive nouns of which *mine* is quickly learned. We also know that children very quickly learn, when they live and grow up in homes where print is evident, that written language is equally effective. In the early years of their literacy experience children come to understand that meaning – information, instructions, stories – comes in two forms: in oral language communication and written communication (and some learn early lessons about other visual forms particularly through computer technology). Sounds and words they have heard and spoken can then be identified in print and, as Adams noted in her famous study in the US, none of this can happen effectively in a vacuum:

> Phonological awareness, letter recognition facility, familiarity with spelling patterns, spelling–sound relations, and individual words must be developed in concert with real reading and real writing and with deliberate reflection on the forms, functions and meanings of texts. (Adams 1990: 422)

Children then are learning important lessons about language very early in their development and without coercion. They are learning to discriminate sounds, recognise patterns in language, develop a working vocabulary, give status to print and make sense of much of the oral and some of the written language in their immediate environments. Children are not passive learners, however. As well as receiving information in these ways, they are also making sense of the ways that they can use spoken and written language to manipulate their worlds and the people in them. The important element to remember here is that children are not achieving this in isolation but in the company of those who also matter to them. The ways that children learn in the complex context of early social relationships in the family is important as they offer lessons for classroom learning. In her seminal work detailing the importance of 'apprenticeship in thinking', Rogoff emphasises:

1. children's active role in making use of social guidance;
2. the importance of tacit and routine arrangements of children's activities and their participation in skilled cultural activities that are not conceived as instructional;

3. cultural variation in both the goals of development and the means by which children achieve a shared understanding with those who serve as their guides and companions through explanation, discussion, provision of expert models, joint participation, active observation and arrangement of children's roles.

(Rogoff 1990: 8)

These three crucial elements involved in the 'guided participation' of Rogoff's theories stress the dual aspect of the frequently acknowledged adult role but also recognise the child's active role in seeking joint participation in their learning, which is simply conceived as social learning or learning that will achieve straightforward, mostly functional, goals.

Box 4.5

- Find out what lessons children have already learned about language by:
  - listening to children talking;
  - listening to children reading;
  - watching children writing and making marks to represent language;
  - asking parents and carers about children's language use at home.
- Acknowledge and discuss variations in dialect.
- Ensure children hear variations through taped stories, poems and visiting authors and storytellers.
- Find a repertoire of stories such as *Toad* by Ruth Brown to extend children's passive and active vocabulary.

Knowledge of texts and authors

The five elements of knowledge for reading described in this chapter are not in any hierarchical order but the expectation is that they will be developed, as in children's homes and other settings before school, alongside each other. We believe that the principle vehicle for ensuring that children develop knowledge for reading is through books and stories, experiencing the joy that they can bring, the emotions they arouse and the warmth and comfort they can offer. We know from research (Meek 1988; David et al. 2000; Grainger et al. 2005) that children's attitudes to literacy are developed through the use of high-quality texts, when even very young children develop favourites and ask for retellings, and older, more experienced readers are drawn into the safety of the worlds created in good books again and again. Experienced adult readers know this feeling too, of feeling safe with particular books and favourite authors.

The love of books starts in infancy with bedtime stories privileged above all else by children and their families and we know that these early experiences with books and stories in emotionally secure contexts influence children's later attitudes to reading (Whitehead 2009). Parents and other family members who read to children and those who tell stories are providing them with strong early lessons about the worth of books and stories and the pleasure of intimate reading collaborations. We cannot be sure, however, that this will be the case for all children and so early encounters with books and stories in schools and classrooms need to replicate and enrich these kinds of early experiences to ensure that all children know what books can be good for. In fact, while some theorists may believe that children who have only had an impoverished early experience of literacy need basic instruction in their early years at school as discussed in a later chapter, Adams, who is often widely quoted as supporting a phonics-first approach, categorically states that this should not be the case:

> Let us begin with the option of withholding connected text until phonic instruction has been completed. Assuming the teaching of two or three correspondences per week and even assuming perfect learning, it would take many years to cover all possible spelling–sound translations. Without the rewards of reading, what child would sit still for such instruction? Without the imminent challenge of reading, what could make it worthwhile? How would the child practice and extend that which had already been taught? (Adams 1998: 272)

The danger in adopting the kind of basics first instruction that Adams is arguing against is that children see phonics as an end in itself and disassociate it from the act of reading. In this way, as Adams so clearly indicates, children may become disaffected and disengaged from reading.

In this book, to encourage, enrich and extend children's knowledge about texts and authors we are proposing a rich reading environment in Chapter 5, high-quality reading resources in Chapter 6 and engaging reading routines in Chapter 7, activities such as frequent reading aloud of high-quality patterned texts, rich and structured narratives in good quality pictures books and repeated readings of favourite authors. The use of multiple copies of the same text will also allow children to indulge in reading favourite stories in the company of their friends. Big books are now so commonly found in classrooms that it seems late in the day to be recommending them, but the quality of the big book must still be the first criterion rather than its size, and children's own independent use of the big book should also be encouraged as well as the teacher's use of it in shared reading times.

Box 4.6

- Ensure that your reading environment contains high-quality texts that will merit reading and many re-readings (see Chapter 5).
- Ensure that your reading resources are of the highest quality and of a good range (see Chapter 6).

(Continued)

(Continued)

- Read aloud and identify authors when doing so, also identifying key features of their work.
- Create intertextual connections between books.
- Encourage children to establish favourite books by supporting re-readings.
- Establish a box of 'Our class favourites' which may change every half term.
- Ensure there are multiple copies of some books.
- Organise the books in author groupings.
- Choose an author of the week.
- Make one quiet reading session into an 'author of the week' read.
- Identify common features of an author's work and make a display of it, with copied illustrations from the book, children's drawings …
- Write to authors, with children or on their behalf.
- Invite authors to visit your school.

Conclusion

In this chapter we have identified the kind of readers that we are hoping children will become in order to define the kind of knowledge they will require. We have looked at the difference between simple instruction in the sounds of letters, the complex understanding of 'symbol systems' described by Goswami (2007) and the very sophisticated layers of knowledge and understanding required in order to be able to read beyond a utilitarian or basic level. We have listed the knowledge that children need as alphabetic knowledge, phonological knowledge, knowledge about the pleasure of reading, knowledge of how books work, knowledge of vocabulary and knowledge about language, and finally, but very importantly, knowledge of texts and authors. We claim that all of this knowledge needs to be gained by children, with free access granted to resources supporting each of them, as one aspect simply will not help children to develop as readers but may instead cause them to be misinformed, misguided or even disaffected.

Further reading

Rogoff, B. (1990) *Apprenticeship in Thinking: Cognitive Development in a Social Context.* New York: Oxford University Press.

Whitehead, M. (2009) *Supporting Language and Literacy Development in the Early Years,* 2nd edn. Maidenhead: Open University Press/McGraw-Hill.

5

Environments for reading

In this chapter we aim:

- to describe cultures of reading and how these may be developed in the classroom;
- to emphasise the importance of positive displays, classroom libraries and reading areas that reflect the ethos and approach to learning in the class and school;
- to demonstrate how discussion can add to a rich culture of reading through literature circles and reading journals;
- to claim how an inclusive and sensitive approach to bilingualism, gender and social class can mean a rich literacy culture, full of difference and similarity and camaraderie.

Everyone who enjoys reading will be able to describe how *where* one reads affects *how* one reads and whether one reads at all. The importance of the reading environment cannot be overestimated. This chapter is all about how teachers can create the kind of environments that will encourage children to want to read and indeed to *feel* like reading. We believe that the desire to read is an intellectual and therefore physical sensation. Readers are often able to describe how they 'feel' like reading: a sensual phenomenon, which triggers the search for one's book and the right space and situation to slake this will to read. School classrooms can be places that help develop these feelings. By offering environments that have the resources, the routines and the ethos that can cater for a range of tastes and dispositions, a culture of reading for pleasure and purpose can be developed. This chapter will explore what teachers can do in schools and classrooms to develop this culture. First, we will say more about developing reading cultures.

Developing a culture of reading

Earlier in this book we discussed how reading is the exclusive ability of human beings who have been described as the 'symbolic species' (Deacon 1997). Goodman (1996) described how learning to read is natural to us, because we are a symbolic species and that we turn to symbolic representations to exploit our ability to make rich and unique meanings about our existence. However, learning to read is not a natural process in the same way as learning to use oral language is natural. The use of written language is relatively too modern an invention, in terms of evolutionary time, to have been wired into our genetic make-up for us to be able to learn it in the same way. Because of the biological support evolution has developed in our brains, we learn oral language just by being exposed to the right forms of inputs and environments (Gee 2004). If learning how to read and write language were natural in this way, most people would learn how do it in the same way most people learn to walk, as walking is biologically supported in the same way as learning oral language.

In this book, we would like to use the word natural to describe the processes of learning to read and write. We believe that it is natural to utilise the rich tools provided by the symbolic representations that written forms of language provide (Goodman 1996). However, learning to read and write – the uses of written language – is also a cultural process. We learn to use and *want* to use these tools when we are immersed in places where reading and writing happens for a purpose and is facilitated by those who are experienced and enthusiastic practitioners. We learn to read and write in environments where it is deemed important, even essential, for a variety of satisfactions to be met. In these circumstances it *seems* natural to want to read. Literacy environments like these make reading and writing a relevant, rich and challenging activity.

Gee (2004: 13) contends that: 'Children who learn to read successfully do so because, for them, learning to read is a cultural and not primarily an instructed process.' Those who successfully learn to read are provided with an environment that contains someone who has mastered reading and who collaborates with the learners in acts that involve reading written texts that the children would not be able to do on their own. It is the model of apprentice and learner again. The learners see reading as not just something which is done to them, because it must be done, but as something which is intrinsic to their emerging identities as readers and as members of a symbolic species. Gee (2004: 13) goes on to say that often school reading is provided by instruction, is a decontextualised process and

> involve[s] practicing skills outside any contexts in which they are used by people who are adept at those skills (e.g. good readers). If this is how children had to learn to play a computer or video game – and, remember, these games are often very long and quite challenging – the games industry would be broke.

Reading cultures can be developed in environments where real readers would want to practise their art. This way, those being inducted into this culture recognise the affordances that these new skills bring and will develop their identities with the support of these new tools. Learning to read as an imposed, alien and pedagogised activity, provided through instruction alone, takes the cultural and apparent 'natural' feeling away from learning to read. A cultural environment of reading where learning to read takes on urgency finds children learning quickly and with pleasure

The following sections of this chapter will describe what teachers can do to develop reading cultures.

Displays

We are great believers that when one walks into a good primary school classroom, the whole environment can immediately 'speak of books and reading'. This has been described earlier in this book as a 'print-rich environment'. The message from the walls, the doors and the corners is 'the teacher and the children in this classroom think that reading is important'. Displays can provide the means to do this as they can celebrate, demonstrate and support the use of language all at the same time. It is hard but satisfying work maintaining vibrant language displays in the classroom, but it is worthwhile for the environment they help to create and learning they support. The classroom displays are fundamentally important for the creation of the cultural identity and ethos of those living therein. The displays can celebrate the diversity, similarity, interests, beliefs, cultures, life styles, enthusiasms and world of the teacher and the children in the classroom. The displays can demonstrate the levels of democracy, harmony, common purpose and inclusivity of what goes on during the school day. The classroom displays reflect all those who live in the classroom space. This makes them fundamental for the development of reading cultures in classrooms.

Classroom displays speak about the ethos of the school and the approach made to learning from the adults. Unfortunately, they can also demonstrate the more traditional hierarchies that have often existed within schools. Classroom walls can be covered with rules of multiple kinds – rules for behaviour and rules for written language are often seen side by side. One could argue that this produces a heavy overemphasis on the encouragement of different forms of discipline, control and compliance. It arguably models a politics of dictatorship, not democracy. In our view, schools should be places that model social democratic and communal values, not top-down heavy control. We would favour displays that reflect the negotiation, dialogue and personal freedoms that can be provided inside these learning spaces and emphasise an ethos of questioning, critique and enquiry. Good displays can demonstrate how the teachers and the school value and model a democracy and a dialogue among those who share the classroom – teachers and children. Sadly, displays can also reflect the enforced anxieties of the teachers and the leaders of the school to hit prescribed and artificial targets made by local and national authorities. Expensive commercial phonics and reading schemes often come with wall charts linked to curriculum levels and the expectations for children working on them. Some classrooms we have seen even publicly log and display individual children's development in reaching these arbitrary levels. Displays of this kind demonstrate for us the break-up of the professionalism of teachers. Outside and often commercial powers are seen to be manipulating the approach the teachers make to teaching and learning, threatening the professional freedom of teachers to make informed decisions in their classes. All this can be learned from classroom displays.

Creating positive displays

When teachers plan their displays, they can learn a great deal from shop windows (Chambers 1991). Shops need to entice the customers, so they organise their displays with great care. Teachers can take note of the materials that are used for the backgrounds, how space is utilised, the way lettering is used. Reading environments need books on display, so bookshop windows are ideal for finding display ideas. When books are displayed, like in bookshops, they must also be available to the customers. Children should be able to borrow the books that are displayed in classrooms. Excited readers will lose patience when they cannot procure the book 'there and then'.

Box 5.1   Ideas for book displays:

- New books
- Books on a theme
- Author of the week
- Illustrator of the week
- Poet of the week
- Alphabet books
- Books related to a topic or an occasion
- Books that have won awards
- Books or magazines that are related to a classroom craze – a video game, sports tournament, television programme, website
- Books translated into other languages/bilingual texts
- Multicultural authors and poets
- Class favourites
- Comics and magazine collections

Displays and phonics

Children can learn about phonology and the structure of words independently when the classroom displays reflect the children's and teacher's interest in words. The best displays are changed regularly and contribute to what is commonly called a 'print-rich' environment. In such an environment, print is used in a purposeful way and for real reasons. Classrooms with labels, rotas, calendars, weather charts, posters related to books, comics and video games demonstrate how words are used and what they look like within real contexts. Displays can be made interactive and the children set challenges.

Box 5.2   Ideas for displays:

- Display environmental print and alphabet charts that have been made by the children.
- Use space to display phrases from books that are the class favourites.
- Display the poems that are known by the class.
- Have alphabets displayed from different languages.
- Make word banks that are linked to the topics the children are studying and demonstrate spelling patterns or word families that are linked to what the children are interested in or are reading at the moment – always link to a familiar context.
- Display the children's own work for the class and visitors to read. Display it low enough for all to have access.
- Have an area for children to comment on the writing of their peers – use Post-it notes.
- Have a debating chart – write an open question linked to a story or something on the news on television to debate. Children are encouraged to state their views by sticking Post-its up on the display.
- Make a list chart – children are encouraged to add to lists of words concerning a topic or a list that demonstrates word rimes or onsets.
- Ask the children to make displays of their own work. An adult can be there to advise. The children can label the display themselves and make decisions about other uses of print.
- Have a set of magnetic letters on a board with which the children can play. The teacher can set a challenge for the children based around letter patterns and word building.

Reading areas and the promotion of reading

Reading is an act 'that has special behavioural needs. We have to set our minds right to do it – to concentrate on the book so that we are drawn inside it and give it our attention' (Chambers 1991: 29). Teachers have found that places in classrooms that are set aside for reading can assist children in finding the right situation for doing it. These places are often called reading areas and become the source for the books that are read inside and outside the classroom. They are also the main area for displays and the promotion of reading.

Classroom libraries, or book areas, are often found in the corner of the room. The space will be carpeted and enclosed by bookshelves. There will be cushions, bean bags or other soft furnishing for places for children to relax with friends and a book. More often than not, book posters will be displayed. In addition to the storage of books, displayed attractively in various pieces of specially designed furniture, there will be story boxes or sacks filled with 'small-world' play figures related to books or the settings of stories. Children can use these with friends. There will also be CD and/or DVD players with headphones and screens. In some classrooms, teachers have widened their conception of literacy and have computers set up with video games for children to play. This will encourage reading from the screen and discussion among the players and observers.

The books in the reading area will be displayed alongside comics and magazines. It is important that children know how to access the reading material they want, have plenty of choice and are given the time to browse. The teacher and the children can label containers, such as plastic peg boxes. Often the teacher will set up the reading area together with the children, deciding on the categorisation of the resources together. Books can be combined by genre, length, speed of reading, familiarity or topic. There will be boxes of magazines and comics. The school may subscribe to some, or the children may bring in their own. The reading areas' resources honour the children's tastes and dispositions – all reading materials are valid and/or open for negotiation.

Book areas should be exciting, inclusive and vibrant areas that form the centrepiece of the reading environment as a whole. The eye should be immediately drawn to this wonderful resource as one walks into the classroom. It should stand like a large art installation dedicated to reading of all kinds and represent the value the whole class has for reading. Teachers often find all sorts of resources to make these areas exciting. Children will enjoy reading in covered areas, so teachers bring in net curtains and drapes to form 'reading camps'. The material is attached to the ceiling and creates a cosy feeling of wonder and escape, which emphasises aspects of the reading experience.

Discussing texts – reading circles/literature circles

Reading circles or literature circles can be an important part of the routine of the school day. They also contribute to the reading environment and culture of the classroom as they encourage discussion about texts.

A literature circle (King and Briggs 2005) is a way to encourage children to read and enjoy talking about books. In most cases, teachers organise a group of children to sit in a circle. They all read the same text and, with the support of their teacher, come together to talk about their reading and to read more of the text together. The circles operate like adult reading groups, where the text is read independently and most of the circle time is spent discussing the groups' responses to the text, with or without the presence of the teacher. For early readers, who are less experienced in their reading, the teacher will often read the text to the children to begin the conversation.

Four or possibly five children in the circle work the best. Larger groups tend to break off into side conversations, and groups with only three members do not seem to have enough energy or diversity of ideas. Teachers can form these first groups making them as heterogeneous as possible by balancing personalities, gender and experience.

How do you get started?

Literature circles can happen in independent reading time, when the other children are engaged in a variety of literacy activities away from the circle. It is important to choose an engaging book that is accessible to all the students. Picture books work well for early readers as they are rich in meaning in both the texts and the illustrations. The first sessions are introductory ones, so it is important to go slowly, providing clear modelling. The teacher can take this opportunity to review his or her own expectations of what might be achieved in the sessions.

In the first session the teacher may hand out the book that has been selected. Teachers often do not allow the children to open them at first. Time may be spent discussing the title, the cover, the contents page and the style of illustrations. The teacher can encourage a general discussion about books, films and other stories that they have read or seen that might be like this one.

With young readers the teacher will often start the reading. This allows the children to hear the 'tune' of the writing. If appropriate for the level of experience in the group, teachers may ask the children to read around the circle. It is important that this kind of group reading does not deteriorate into a Victorian school model of reading instruction. Teachers should not insist that all the children read. When everyone who wants to has had the chance to read, depending on reading and writing experience, the teacher could ask the children to jot down in their reading journals (see below) what they are thinking about the book at that moment. Allow them time to discuss what they have written with a neighbour. For very young children the oral discussion would be quite enough.

When the teacher is reading young children can be encouraged to join in with repeated words and rhymes. They can be asked to discuss the story, making connections with their own lives or other stories that they know. The teacher may want to use a 'big book' with the group and encourage the children to read along at certain points in the texts and discuss the construction of words and phrases. However, all this needs to be carried out with an emphasis on meaning-making (Medwell et al. 1998). Literature circles have a different emphasis and agenda than guided reading (see Chapter 7) which is more concerned with planned and specific teaching. Literature circles encourage pleasure in discussion and the sharing of meanings in small groups.

Depending upon the children's experience in the circle, at a certain point in the session, time can be provided for children to read on their own – perhaps setting a question for them to think about. It should be an open-ended question

In subsequent sessions you may wish to try brainstorming to launch discussions. The children can be asked to take the book away to read with their parents or friends or on their own.

Reading journals

Reading journals (King and Briggs 2005) are notebooks within which children jot down their responses to their reading as they read. These responses can be to the book they are reading in the literature circles, but they also may be responding to books that have been read in story times or at home with their parents or siblings. Children can be encouraged to be honest and to use expressive language. The teacher can keep her own reading journal and use it as a model for the class. The children may choose to illustrate characters in their reading journals, rewrite endings or add bits they consider to be missing from the story. Some children like to draw maps, pictures and diagrams to sort out journeys, events and relationships. They may also want to record the names and details of characters as they appear in the story.

An important aspect of reading journals is the communication – and consequently the relationship that is built up through joint discussions about the books that being read – between the teacher and the child. This helps the development of a successful reading culture in the environment of the classroom. The teacher should respond regularly to what the children are writing in their journals. They should develop a dialogue with the children, but they must not correct what the children have said or comment on spelling, etc. The emphasis within this dialogue is on the sharing of human responses. The more traditional strict and hierarchical relationships between the teacher and child in schools can be broken down by this dialogue. Both contributors to the discussion are writing as people who both share an interest in the stories being read.

Box 5.3   When reading a book what should the children be doing?

- Bringing their own experiences to the text to make sense of it.
- Predicting what might happen next, and why, to help them structure their reading by looking for clues in the text and to make them want to read on.
- Sharing their rich mental pictures to help them learn from each other how to do this.
- Empathising by saying what they feel about the characters to identify with them.

- Assessing what makes them keep reading and to articulate what makes a good story.
- Evaluating why the text is like it is and why it works to help them develop critical reading skills.
- Seeking clarification and re-reading to realise the significance of particular words.
- Comparing events and characters with those in other stories or films.
- Identifying themes and ideas to make a wider sense of their reading.
- Discussing spelling patterns – onsets and rimes.
- Asking questions to clarify their thinking, become critical readers and help them become involved in the text.

Book owners

When we read books we invest a great deal of emotion in them. This is why keen readers tend to be book buyers. Book covers can be very attractive and remind us of the stories, settings, events and characters. Book shelves full of books say much about the person to whom they belong. They often indicate that books are an intrinsic part of a reading culture and a culture interested in stories. Some people's homes have shelves filled with DVDs and books. This, too, tells a tale about the extent to which the owners feel like hearing and/or seeing stories. When one owns books it enables re-reading and re-reading can foster deeper understanding of the meaning of the texts and a greater knowledge of the author's and illustrator's style and approach. Books on the shelves can give pleasure as they represent and actually contain the source of satisfaction we have had in the past reading them and pleasures that one can look forward to having again when they are re-read. Perhaps e-books can give the same feelings of satisfaction as one electronically scrolls down the titles – that remains to be seen, but for the moment, having books on the shelves contributes to a reading culture.

Schools can encourage children to have books at home by selling books in school. There are plenty of book clubs that sell books to children in schools via attractive catalogues. Many schools have a book stall that sells both new and second-hand. These are often run by parents and the children and can become a regular centre where children and parents can meet to talk about books and make those very powerful recommendations. Book stalls can have regular promotion events for authors, poets or genres of books. It is also a way of encouraging the parents and teachers to buy books, by having a section for 'older readers'.

There are also book fairs that regularly can be brought into school. These can be part of a week when reading, stories and books take an extra special place in the timetable of the school. An author, poet or storyteller can be invited in to talk about and read their work. They may even be asked to work alongside the children and share their enthusiasm and experience for writing with the children teachers and parents.

Gender and other issues

Involving the whole school community in literacy activities makes the culture of reading come alive.

Gender has become a greater issue now for teachers in schools, particularly when teachers are told to assess literacy development by testing at specific ages. It can be argued that measurable outcomes in education have been given greater emphasis and that when a school's results are made more public in the form of league tables of schools which seek to compare the 'performance' of the children and teachers, results between girls and boys will inevitably show a disparity (Moss 2005). Boys' weaker performance in reading and writing in the school years has often been an issue that has been debated. Any gender disparities that have been noticed in data have been largely explained from a biological basis – boys' comparative late development (Millard 1997). Yet now, the current public and media exposure of outcomes from tests has contributed to teachers being told by governments to redouble their efforts to create more parity between boys' and girls' achievement at specific ages. The government argument is that the 'education product' must be improved for boys. A new managerial approach insists on 'quality outcomes' based on targets. For governments, biological explanations no longer will do (Moss 2005) even though there may be truth in them – boys and girls may develop in literacy at different rates, which age-specific expectations of progress will only expose. Yet one is also inclined to ask: 'which boys?' and 'which girls?' Might the differences in achievement and development in literacy be more acute between children from different socio-economic backgrounds? One needs to proceed with caution when making an analysis of the difference between boys' and girls' development as readers and writers, and look for other more significant reasons for patterns of underachievement.

Despite the debates over gender, potential readers are fostered when the people they know around them are reading too. This means encouraging all members of families to be involved in literacy cultures – men too. Schools sometimes make great efforts to provide male reader role models for boys in school. For example, in a school where one of the authors taught, the reserve side of a local football team was encouraged to come into school. Much to the footballers' surprise, instead of coaching the sport, they came into classrooms in independent reading times and read alongside the children. In another case we have heard of, a grandfather was asked to sit in the entrance area of the school and simply read as the children were arriving at school in the morning! There is little clear research evidence to demonstrate the effectiveness of this particular kind of initiative, but it does indicate the efforts of schools to tackle what is perceived as a problem with boys and reading.

The activities in the box that involve language and stories can be promoted for all children in the school.

Box 5.4   Ideas for encouraging reading for all:

- Involve males and females from outside the school in literacy activities in the school from all social classes.
- Involve more males in reading activities in the school – older boys, male teachers, fathers, male visitors.
- Encourage fathers to come to parent consultations.
- Carefully select texts that will appeal to all children from all social classes and ethnic backgrounds.
- Use texts that draw on popular culture – use comics and magazines alongside books.
- Ensure that other texts are valued in the class – DVDs, TV, CDs, video games, websites.
- Carefully balance fiction and non-fiction. Do not assume that boys only like non-fiction!
- Ensure support for, and discussions with, boys to foster independence in reading.
- Make sure there are plenty of books that use dialect. It is important that children see some books that use their home dialects too.
- Have taped stories that reflect the linguistic variety of the class, the community and the nation as a whole.

Bilingualism

In creating a reading culture in classrooms, book collections will need to reflect the home background of the children. Fortunately, there are many very good books that do this. Books can reflect a variety of cultural contexts. Bilingual learners will be assisted when there are books that reflect the cultural contexts with which they identify.

In addition to books reflecting a variety of cultural contexts, classrooms will also contain texts written in children's home/community languages. Children will learn that reading in school and outside is not only about reading in English. Teachers will often ensure that they are fully informed about the language experiences of all the children in their class. They are aware of the children's ability to speak, read or write home languages and encourage children to use and develop these skills in the classroom. Books written in home/community languages can be taken home to encourage children's use of them with their parents and siblings. Dual-language books enable children and parents to make comparisons between the two languages and encourage conversation about language.

Like all children learning to read, there should be plenty of opportunities for bilingual learners to hear English stories read aloud. Listening is an effective way to learn. Storytimes when children gather just to listen to stories must be a regular fixture. Listening areas in classrooms facilitate independent learning too. The use of dual language tapes and books makes these periods of time with CDs and headphones rich in learning.

Book-making is important for all children learning to read. Asking bilingual learners to make their own books using their own language is a wonderful opportunity to learn about language. The children can be supported by teachers and teaching assistants, by children with different language abilities and also by parents who share the home/community language with the children. The books can retell favourite stories or be non-fiction texts. Perhaps they provide information about their home country or their community. Encouraging children to interrogate the scripts of different languages will help develop an interest in words and languages that will lead to greater understanding of their mother tongue.

Activities that involve other children from various linguistic backgrounds create rich opportunities for using and learning a language. Bilingual learners can be provided with opportunities to discuss topics in their home language or English or both. Reading cultures can develop when the whole class feel their language and their language experiences are valued and group activities that combine these different languages promote such a culture.

Social class

We know from research (for example, Smith et al. 1997; Becket 2000; McCallum and Redhead 2000; Thomas 2000, DfEE 2000; DfES 2004) that levels of economic prosperity and social class are the greatest predictors of educational success or failure in school.

> Those from higher socio-economic groups do significantly better at each stage of our system than those from lower ones – indeed socio-economic group is a stronger predictor of attainment than ability. (DfES 2004: 20)

Many have argued (Bernstein 1996; Lambirth 2007a) that some of the reasons for underachievement among poorer, disadvantaged working-class children can be associated with the 'social class assumptions' of the pedagogy employed within the school – that the culture in classrooms is constructed, maintained and dominated by the middle class.

Everything that we have suggested in this chapter is intended to emphasise the importance of inclusive environments within which children can learn. However, we want to repeat our argument that teachers need to be aware of their own cultural background and the many assumptions and values that come with it. Books for us may seem to be the source of much of our own joy and satisfaction in life, but for some, they may not have the same appeal. Literacy activities (including reading) are related to the culture within which they occur and so teachers cannot assume that all children will want to engage with books equally. Therefore a culture has to be created in classrooms that welcomes all and makes efforts to link the literacy activities on offer in school with the literacy activities of all the home backgrounds of the children in the class.

Teachers and children need to know each other. Teachers and children need to know and appreciate each other too (Gale and Densmore 2000). There should be an active trust, a mutuality and a negotiated authority within the classroom that involves a sharing of different cultural perspectives with an attempt to understand.

> Teachers also need to create opportunities to get to know their students and for their students to get to know them and themselves. The chance to give and receive in this way is generally advanced through open discussions that give respect to others' traditions and histories. Through these kinds of supportive relations with their teachers, students can be encouraged to develop their interests and abilities. (Gale and Densmore 2004: 147)

Children need to feel that their own culture and social class background is respected in school and that there is genuine interest from teachers and fellow pupils. Of course, as we have already mentioned, tests of culturally specific levels of literacy development work against this form of relationship building, as pressures are exerted on teachers and children to meet these demands at specific ages. Pressures like these are political in nature. Indeed, schools cannot by themselves change the injustice caused by the distinctions between class and power and the subsequent relations in society. Nevertheless, teachers and children can discuss these issues while getting to understand each other – perceiving the similarities and differences that social class and culture can foster. It is this analysis of society by a close community of teachers and children that gives classrooms a huge potential for subversive social power. If teachers begin to create democratic environments in their classrooms with children from an early age, schools can become centres of social justice and equality. With a more negotiated and equitable environment to learn within, children will feel more comfortable and better equipped to learn.

Box 5.5   Getting to know each other:

- Have half-termly reading conferences with children, either one-to-one or in pairs – talk to them about their interests e.g. gaming, books, magazines, TV, internet activities.
- Arrange meetings with the parents to talk about the children's interests and pastimes.
- Make active and meaningful use of children's literacy practices as a resource for the curriculum – encourage them to bring in games, magazines, other texts of interest and incorporate them into the work you want to do with the children.

(Continued)

(Continued)

- Organise trips to a variety of different venues, events and environments that cross cultural lines.
- Create displays and exhibitions that honour and celebrate children's home life and home literacy practices.
- Ensure the book collections in the school and classroom reflect the social classes and cultural backgrounds of the children.
- Encourage children to keep electronic or pen-and-paper journals that enable them to write freely about their own experiences inside and outside the classroom.
- Organise parents to come in to celebrate the children's work at different times during the day.
- Ensure there are regular times when teachers and children can share their enthusiasm for different forms of texts or activities from home.
- Embed popular culture into school literacy practices.

Conclusion

In this chapter, we have tried to emphasise the importance of creating a welcoming and inclusive environment for all children in our classrooms. When efforts are made in this way, learning to read becomes a great deal easier. Reading, like all learning when it is at its best, is a social activity and constructing a caring and exciting environment for children to learn will build an important foundation for the rest of teaching to occur.

Further reading

Chambers, A. (1991) *The Reading Environment*. Stroud: Thimble Press.
Gee, J.P. (2004) *Situated Language Learning: A Critique of Traditional Schooling*. Abingdon: Routledge.

6

Resources for reading

In this chapter we aim:

- to demonstrate that resources for reading include time and space;
- to show how resourcing for reading includes attention to resourcing for writing;
- to emphasise that teachers, adults and those in the wider community can be an invaluable resource for reading as they mediate texts, model reading for pleasure and to access information, demonstrate aspects of reading and initiate children into reading behaviours and habits;
- To include children, friends, peers and older children as helpful resources for developing readers as they share their own enjoyment of books and stories and their own developing knowledge of how language and print work.

The central focus for a reading classroom is the provision of an ample stock of well-organised and well-presented children's literature, stories and high-quality texts across genres. However, this chapter will begin with classroom provision around this to ensure that books and texts of all kinds are surrounded by a print-rich environment that will support children's developing knowledge of the alphabet and the codes and symbols that combine to make the print version of the English language. It will then work towards the idea of a rich reading area. In addition, the necessary resources of space, time and adult help also need careful planning. While resources for reading, writing and speaking and listening will be identified, further consideration of the interconnectedness of these three modes will be considered in greater detail in a later chapter.

Time for reading

Time is a valuable resource which recently has been sadly squeezed and heavily reduced in relation to reading in schools. The introduction of the National Strategies in 1998 created Literacy Hours in schools. One of the worrying side effects of this was that all activities traditionally associated with this broad umbrella term 'literacy', that is reading, writing and speaking and listening, were all tightly regulated and contained within this single hour of each day. The enormous demands of a heavily overloaded and carefully timetabled primary curriculum meant that many teachers felt that they could now ill afford quiet reading times for children or read-aloud times at various times of the day. If reading did not happen within the Hour then often it did not happen at all. Within the Hour, of course, there has only ever been time in some classes for extracts of texts to be shared with the whole class or read independently or in small groups.

This was not the case in all classes and with all teachers. Some have persisted in their practice of finding time for reading whole books in one or a series of sittings and have worked creatively to find time for children to read alone or in the company of others for significant periods of time. Some teachers have continuously forged time in their busy timetables to read aloud to children during and/or at the end of each and every day. These teachers are to be congratulated for their confidence, knowledge and understanding of how reading and readers must be supported. However, now following a succession of government initiatives (for example, Excellence and Enjoyment and the Primary Strategy) there have been new freedoms introduced to teachers to enable them to achieve literacy objectives across the curriculum and to use time more creatively. Of course the new primary curriculum will raise even more possibilities within the statutory framework.

There have been many critics of the way that literacy teaching has been managed in schools. Notably, Whitehead called for commitment to a '24-hour literacy' describing this kind of literacy as 'a shared human cultural experience, not an ordeal' (Whitehead 1999: 59). She continues:

> Very young children, who are just starting to read, write and understand symbols of all kinds, children who initially speak and understand languages other than English and children who have difficulties with school literacy, are not criminals and do not deserve to be terrorised, nor can they be coerced into literacy. (Whitehead 1999: 53)

Whitehead understood that interest, pleasure and engagement are crucial ingredients for all children learning to read and that time is required to help children understand their own literacy beginnings, consolidate existing learning and build bridges between this and new learning as well as new ways of learning. Some children of course need more time than others and cannot be part of the quick-wins culture expected of them in school. Could this be why some children underachieve or achieve less in the time frame allowed than others? It may also help to explain why European colleagues have decided that formal schooling and instructional practices should begin at least a year or two later than here in England, to allow time for children to develop, to make connections between early print experiences and new symbol-making opportunities and to learn at a pace suitable for them while they are young.

Box 6.1   Time is pressured now in primary classrooms but time must be found for children to:

- Explore alphabets, writing resources and book resources
- Browse
- Share texts with friends
- Listen to stories and books
- Read quietly alone
- Puzzle over books
- Sometimes re-read favourite books
- Write own books
- Choose what to read
- Hear stories read aloud

Space for reading

Classrooms, like timetables, in primary education are busy spaces and teachers are pulled in many directions as they account for their use of space for different curriculum areas. However, there are essential elements of a primary classroom necessary to promote reading and literacy, essential in consolidating and extending home and outside school experiences and an absolute requirement to support the significant amount of children in our schools who have not experienced the pleasure and power of literacy, reading and story or had print mediated for them in their worlds prior to or outside of school. Space is necessary to display and promote books and other texts, for children to comfortably browse and for pairs and groups of children to engage in book 'gossip' (Chambers 1993). Space is also required for the kinds of resources described in this chapter: alphabetic/dictionary/word book displays, writing areas, listening corners, children's own display areas for reviews, book covers, advertisements for books, space for children's work about books to be displayed, questions about books and role on the wall activities. Display space is also important for word walls and all the other kinds of vocabulary displays needed to immerse children in print and to encourage them to become curious about language, for example all the 'muddy' words in *Mr Gumpy's Motor Car*, 'words we like' displays, words for example like *serendipity* or *onomatopoeia* so that from the earliest age in school children can both feel interesting words on their lips and see how they are written.

Box 6.2   Space in the classroom should be provided:

- For a well organised book area
- For children to sit alone or with friends
- So that children can listen to audio-taped stories or poems
- To make it easy for children to write
- To make books
- For children to display their writing
- For displays of books, e.g. favourite book of the week, books on a particular topic ...
- For displays of activities in relation to books

Print lessons

There is no doubt that children need information about our alphabet, how it works, what it looks like in varying forms and how it already relates to their known lives, for example children's own names and the names of people they know. Children arrive in school already informed to varying levels about different aspects of the alphabetic world. Some children will have heard nursery rhymes, had books shared with them, had help to write their names, write party invitations and thank you letters. Even without such helpful mediation children live and grow currently in our society in England in a print filled world. Babies are surrounded by print from birth in every corner of their environment: the streets along which prams and buggies are pushed contain advertising hoardings; there are advertisements on buses; shop names are in extra large print; all shopping bags seem to carry logos and shop names; roads are full of street furniture addressing drivers and pedestrians, giving street names, directions and traffic signs and warnings; clothes carry print and logos. At home, food packaging is print-full; all bought products are packaged with print labels. Books are designed and constructed with babies in mind, for example tiny-sized books, books that make sounds, textured feely books, board books, waterproof bath-time books and books to hang on cot and pram sides. Babies and young children in our society are immersed from birth into this world of print and will inevitably by chance, or by mediated design and parental intervention, absorb information from it because early lessons from parents and families teach them that print matters in everyday lives. Also, in England it is common practice to draw children's attention to environmental print at very early stages, although it seems this is not the case in other European countries (David et al. 2000).

Classrooms then need to acknowledge these early and outside learning experiences and mirror elements of environmental print in order to build on the connections that children have begun to make between the symbolic world around them and meaning-making in real and semi-authentic classroom contexts. Signs and notices constructed by teachers and children and carrying authentic messages are an important element of this. Resources to support children in constructing these themselves are important and so carry-boxes or toolboxes containing fat felt pens, strips of card, Blu-tack, masking tape and scissors will both carry meaningful prompts and support children in using appropriate materials for appropriate purposes. Through the use of emergent literacy practices, children begin to organise their developing phonological understanding into print forms. Very quickly children learn that print symbols carry meaning and that they make a difference to action: the lesson learned is that print is effective for a range of purposes and for various audiences. Children learn this, not through instruction as we said earlier, but through modelled practice and through experience of the impact that print has on its audiences. Constructing such messages and labels helps young children to draw together their developing knowledge of the sounds they hear in their worlds and the symbols they are beginning to realise represent those sounds. The connections between emergent writing and children's developing ability to read print are very strong.

Alphabet resources

Alphabets now come in a range of styles, shapes and materials. It is possible to buy large wooden or plastic alphabet letters, magnetic letters, letters that stick to glass, pastry cutter letters, roll and write alphabets to help with direction in letter writing, alphabet jigsaws – and I am sure there will be others not listed here as well as those that inventive teachers construct themselves. Some teachers make fabric, textured alphabet books or friezes to support children and of course there are many commercially produced alphabet friezes currently available. In their everyday classroom environments, young children need full and constant access to this kind of physical support for their learning in order to explore, rehearse and perform activities in playful ways. Alphabet books should also be provided and co-constructed with children. Commercially produced texts are fun to include in a specially designed alphabet area and can include now favourite storybook character alphabets, food alphabets, animal alphabets, name alphabets and so on . . . and these are a far cry from the very traditional Ladybird alphabet books of the past. Children also enjoy browsing Richard Scary-type alphabet texts.

Box 6.3 Alphabet Knowledge can be promoted through the creation of an alphabet area which could include:

- Physical letter shapes for drawing around, exploration and play:
  - wooden or plastic letters
  - magnetic letters
  - stick-on-glass letters
  - pastry cutter letter shapes

(Continued)

(Continued)

- Alphabet books:
  - textured books (sandpaper/fabric)
  - class-constructed alphabet books
  - class name books
  - book character alphabets
  - food alphabets
  - dictionaries and other word books

- Alphabet friezes:
  - commercially produced friezes
  - class-constructed alphabet pictures forming a frieze

- Alphabet jigsaw puzzles
- Alphabet building blocks

Commercially produced word books and dictionaries now come in a variety of guises and a range of these which may appeal to different children's interests and abilities needs to be made available for children's continuous access. There are very specialised dictionaries for young readers created with children in mind but in addition children also need to become familiar with the kind of everyday dictionary that adults use and in fact they are able to find their way through these surprisingly quickly, particularly with the help of playful activities and a supportive older child or adult.

Writing resources

In a book about teaching reading it is important to also include resources for writing as we know how closely the two literacy activities are entwined in children's developing understanding of phonology, phonemes and graphic representations. Writing and reading their own name in a variety of ways and using all sorts of materials is a constantly developing and highly engaging activity for children and a good indicator of their stage of understanding in relation to symbolic representation (see Kress 1997: 66 for a full discussion in relation to name writing). As well as free access to writing materials, children will also need to see opportunities for their name signs to be used and celebrated, for example on models and pictures or on home-made 'snap' cards. The important point about resources for writing is that they are freely available to children and they are wide-ranging in content. For example, if children want to make a label or notice then card is available with fat felt pens with which to write. If children intend making and authoring books, then book-making materials such as split pins, hole punchers, treasury tags and appropriately sized paper are there for them. Important too is the idea of transportability, that is if the child has made a huge model from blocks and is intent on labelling it then to have a simple carry-box of materials to take to the model makes this task simple, convenient and efficient. In the adult world we have choices about writing materials and have learned about the appropriate use of these from experience. Offering choices to children facilitates their induction into the adult world of writing to make meaning. For example, the choice of whether to send a note on a Post-it sticker for speed and efficiency or to craft a letter on headed paper is dependent on a range of factors, one of which is the relationship between the writer and the reader. And if you wish your writing to be read and to be given significance then how it is presented is of course important. Providing Post-it stickers, books and paper of all sizes, shapes, colours and textures may feel like a luxury but is in fact an important part of introducing children to the contemporary world of literacy which some, but not all, may already have met in part at home before and outside of school contexts. In addition, motivating children to write becomes less of an issue than if they are confined to writing in exercise books with non-descript pencils.

Box 6.4   A Writing area promoting mark-making, writing and authoring will help children to understand the connection between the two and help to develop their phonological understanding. It should include at least:

- Varieties of pens and pencils
- A range of paper and card
- Book-making materials and small, made books
- Individual white boards
- One or more computers
- Flip chart on easel
- A collection of physical alphabet materials
- Chalk and wet paintbrushes for outside use
- Posters and examples of written script
- Name cards
- Carry-boxes of pens, pencils, paper and card to transport to other areas

---

Books and other print texts

It is troubling to see that a recent government sponsored review (Rose 2006) has promoted the idea of easily decodable books as being appropriate for young children. In an age where books are competing with screen texts and struggling to find a place in many young children's lives, it seems to us to be more than ever important to raise the profile of high-quality children's books and stories.

The primary school is the perfect context in which to promote the range and variety of books to children. Teachers have the perfect opportunity to model the pleasure, the humour and the potential for deep engagement that is possible through books and other printed texts. In the rich world of children's publishing now it is easily possible to cater for all children's interests and passions, to demonstrate the intertextual potential of books, to show children how some authors can be trusted to share worlds with us again and again in safe ways, in familiar patterns and in different stories, to help children to access other parts of the world through beautifully illustrated and crafted stories, traditional tales and non-fiction books, to help children to see how some texts have patterns and repeated shapes or predictable rhymes.

Not all print texts fit the traditional form, however, but still they will be important to include in a carefully constructed book area. The use of comics in school contexts is often contested and comic books, football magazines, annuals, catalogues and other texts from popular culture can frequently be found relegated to a 'wet play box' as if they constitute second-rate reading material unworthy of gaining the status of the reading area. We believe that such reading material often has merit, in that children are motivated to read them, they often range across writing genres, many provide useful lessons about print and how it can be used creatively and for authentic purposes and, importantly, they can be effective in creating a real bridge between home and school cultures for literacy.

Box 6.5   The book corner should be sufficiently inviting to be seen as a prize place to be in the classroom, a place which children plead to be allowed to occupy! It should include:

- Picture books (in all primary classes)
- Extended texts (from reception)
- Information texts
- Big books
- Multiple copies of some texts
- Poetry anthologies
- Comics
- Magazines (e.g. computer magazines, football magazines)
- Catalogues
- Displays of book covers
- Book reviews by children and adults
- Displays of activities related to books
- Displays of class favourites
- Cushions and comfortable places to sit
- A space to listen to audio-taped stories

Picture books

It is difficult to believe that there are any teachers or educators who are unaware now of the value of picture books. A chapter discussing appropriate resources for reading would be impoverished without a strong focus on the centrality of picture books in children's reading development. We know from research that reading picture fiction is infectious and that siblings and families can often be induced to join in when good stories are being read at home. We know too that this kind of reading behaviour at home has long-lasting effects on children's reading development and reading habits (Whitehead 2009). What is it specifically then that high-quality picture fiction can offer? Whitehead summarises it in the following ways.

1. They require that very young children behave like active readers.
2. Picture books start the literary habit of helping readers to make connections between books and life.
3. Experiences with picture books teach most of the basic literary conventions: beginnings and ways in to narrative; plot complications, problems and challenges; the resolving of difficulties and happy endings.
4. They have small and manageable examples of print.
5. Picture books play a complex and significant part in introducing children to literature and preparing them for literacy.

(Whitehead 2009: 48)

Whitehead, M. *Supporting Language and Lieracy Development in the Early Years*, Second edition © 2009, McGraw-Hill. This material is reproduced with the kind permission of the Open University.

Of course we also know that good picture books operate at many levels and engage readers of varying levels, from infant to adult if they are good enough. In her celebration of *Cracking Good Picture Books*, a play on words in itself, Graham claims that with extraordinary picture books 'you can read it and find you can still possess it, particularly perhaps in your visual memory ... but also in your aural memory' (Graham 2004: 1). She suggests that there will be many adults who are able to recall the entire written text of Sendak's *Where the Wild Things Are* and now of course the new film version will ensure that this timeless story impacts on even more generations of readers. With such strong inventive, meaning-based, visual texts children have the enormous task of contributing to the story and filling in the gaps left between the illustrations and the print, taking on the task as the proliferate 'seekers after meaning' (Wells 1986: 43) that they seem to be designed to be. The job of simply decoding the print text is rather a small and undemanding one, leaving meaning-making as central, just as it should be.

Information texts

As already established, children are great 'seekers after meaning' and this is particularly evident in their voracious appetite from an early age for information texts as well as familiar storybooks. In the very earliest years this may take the form of naming books, but children are interested to find more about their own lives as well about objects of their own interest. And so books such as the Ahlburg's *Baby Catalogue* and Nick Sharratt and Pippa Goodhart's *You Choose* need to sit alongside information books about dinosaurs, wild animals, other countries and so on. The wonderfully illustrated, wordless text *Window* by Jeanie Baker and *Dear Greenpeace* by Simon James are two further examples of the ways in which information texts and stories cross boundaries and seamlessly interconnect.

Popular cultural texts

While some educators may be concerned about including non-book texts in their book areas, we feel strongly that children need to see texts reflected in their lives and texts that matter to them in their outside school lives also given status in their classrooms. We are encouraged by the fact that authors with the reputation of, for example, Jeremy Strong and Lauren Child have contributed their stories for television screening. We would therefore include comics, magazines for children and catalogues and listings, as well as the opportunity for children to access stories, games and activities related to stories, websites and other texts on computer screens. However, it is important to carefully scrutinise all such texts and ensure that they reach the same high standards and meet similar criteria for quality that would be applied to other book-based texts. The inclusion of these texts would increase children's motivation, make links with out-of-school literacies, help children to look for literacy beyond books, satisfy children's wide-ranging interests and provide wide-ranging genres to browse and from which children can make choices.

Box 6.6   How do you assess texts for inclusion in your classroom to ensure quality?

- Do you know exactly what you have included in your book provision?
- Have you read all or most of the books there?
- Are there any books about which you have concerns?
- What have you decided to do about those?
- Do you have favourite stories/books in the book area?
- What do you think makes a good picture book?
- How many picture books do you enjoy re-reading to your class?

- What do you know about the different roles played by the illustrations in picture books?
- Have you assessed your text provision for any issues related to gender, class and race?
- How many stories do you have where female characters take the lead?
- How many books or other text provision have you included that mirror other ethnicities?
- How are children and their families and communities represented in the book provision you have chosen?
- What role does humour play in the books/stories you have chosen to include?
- Have you included a good range of poetry and poetic texts, information books, multiple copies of favourite texts, including comics and magazines, big books, very small books, collections by favourite authors?

People (and especially people who read)

The role of the teacher in choosing and disseminating resources to support children in all aspects of learning to read is without doubt a fundamental role. The nature of the resources chosen and the ways in which these are made accessible to children is heavily dependent on individual teachers' knowledge (discussed in detail in Chapter 3). Whitehead refers to the role of significant adults in children's early literacy development as including acting as literacy informants, literacy demonstrators, scribes, reading partners, models and facilitators (Whitehead 2009: 79). In other chapters we have used Gregory's term 'literacy brokers' to refer to those people at home who support children in their early reading and we have extended this term to refer to teachers as 'professional literacy brokers' in school contexts. In this way we are trying to redefine the role of teachers and other adults in the classroom beyond that of instructor or disseminator of print information to also include other aspects. In the context of this chapter relating to resources we see the inclusion of people who act as mediators between children and texts as a key factor.

The very distinct roles of teachers have been discussed earlier and should include a range of teaching strategies. We firmly believe that teachers bear a very heavy responsibility for demonstrating, sharing with and fostering a love of books and stories in the children they encounter in schools. In order to do this successfully, we also claim that teachers themselves must become voracious readers of books at their own level as well as of children's literature. This cannot be compromised. Teachers must read to children, share books with children, include read-aloud sessions in their plans and guard such sessions against erosion. Traditionally, additional adults have been invited into classrooms to listen to children read. In the new culture of the literacy hour, some of this practice has disappeared. We are arguing in this book for other adults to be frequently invited into schools and classrooms for the single most important reason – reading to and with children, individually and in small groups. There is a huge resource for this inclusion in local communities, where, as well as parents and family members, there are other responsible adults who can with support learn or re-learn the skill of enjoying books and oral stories with children. The rewards from this are many and include:

- another voice, dialect, accent for children to hear;
- an additional time for children to share an intimate session with a book and a mediating adult;
- more rehearsal time for children to engage with print in the company of a supportive adult, without anxiety and the fear of being tested;
- a time for nursery rhymes, jingles, poetry to be shared and heard;
- an opportunity to play with books, sounds, language.

As we have discovered earlier, for those children who have had in any sense an impoverished (or no) introduction to the joy to be found in language, stories and books, this kind of 'lesson' is the best that can be provided and far exceeds any benefit to be gained from direct instruction or drilling (see Adams 1990; Whitehead 2009). The essential requirement for any adult participating in such activities is that they themselves enjoy language, stories and books and are able to impart this to children in their company.

Peers and other children who read

Children learn lessons from each other very effectively and in the following chapter we will discuss in more detail examples of routines such as reading circles where children engage in activities that will support other children in reading. In these early stages, children are generally very good at displaying their own knowledge and helping other children around them to both read and write. It is important at the beginning of their school experience to nurture this inclination in children and to encourage support activities. And so, planning opportunities for children to read, to browse and to share books in pairs and in small groups is an essential element of the reading classroom. Children quickly come to enjoy being a resource for other readers and will readily demonstrate their own developing knowledge of print as their peers are heard to struggle or grapple with sounds. Book buddies is a scheme that many teachers already employ, where older children are invited into a class of less experienced readers to share books and tell stories and this is always popular with both groups of children and often particularly popular and useful for those older children who have come to read later or are still learning print lessons. Older, inexperienced readers invariably benefit enormously from such additional opportunities to hone their skills.

Grouping children is a sensitive and sometimes a contentious issue. We believe that confining children to groups of the same or similar ability in reading, while sometimes being useful, can also be counterproductive if the groups are static. Enthusiastic readers are able to model both the act of reading as well as positive attitudes to reading and so we would encourage a mixture of ability groupings, friendship groupings and mixed-ability groupings through each week to ensure that children have the opportunity to benefit from the company of a range of other readers.

Conclusion

In this chapter we have identified the wide range of resources that we feel is essential in a reading classroom, particularly in the early years but also throughout the primary stages. As well as considering practical ideas for reading and writing resources, we have also given consideration to the inclusion of the resources of time and space in developing high-quality reading provision. We have argued for a wide range of texts to be included as well as books in the knowledge that this will both motivate children and help to build links between home and out-of-school literacy activities and new school literacy. As we are keenly aware that many of the lessons that children learn about print are from their emergent writing activities (further discussed in Chapter 8) we make a plea for writing resources to be of a high quality and readily available for children, and transportable to all classroom areas so that children can use writing for their own purposes and in support of other activities. Additionally we have attended to the Vygotskian notion of more knowledgeable others supporting children in working towards their 'zone of proximal development' and discussed how people, adults and children can be helpful to inexperienced readers.

Further reading

Graham, J. (2004) *Cracking Good Picture Books: Teaching Literature at Key Stage 1.* Sheffield: NATE.
Gregory, E. and Williams, A. (2004) 'Living literacies in homes and communities', in T. Grainger (ed.), *The RoutledgeFalmer Reader in Language and Literacy.* Abingdon: RoutledgeFalmer.

7

Reading routines

In this chapter we aim:

- to celebrate the joy and the importance of reading aloud and how it contributes to children's learning about the sounds of words and letters;
- to emphasise how independent reading can help children learn about reading in a collaborative and social environment;
- to stress the affordances of shared and guided reading;
- to demonstrate the importance of one-to-one reading.

In this chapter we discuss how the environment and resources for reading can be used on a daily basis in the form of regular activities and events that will promote, model and teach reading in early years classrooms. Once again we will be drawing on the principles of teaching and learning developed by Rogoff et al. (2001) to highlight education as an act of participation and not something which is always done to you (Marshall 1998). We will be describing ways of using shared, guided and independent reading to teach both the processes and strategies of reading. We begin by exploring reading aloud and its sister activity, independent reading times.

Reading aloud

There is strong evidence that being read to is an essential element in learning to read (Durkin 1966; Clarke 1976; Wells 1986). The writers of this book feel passionately that 'story time' is an explicit form of teaching reading. It would be a mistake to conceptualise it as an exotic luxury within a packed school day. Instead, it should be seen as an essential element of the reading curriculum (Grainger and Tod 2000). As we have mentioned earlier, we often hear from students and teachers that the read-aloud time, a time when all the children gather to hear and share the experience and processes of great storytelling, is being squeezed out of the day, that it is no longer being given a privileged space in timetables. Perhaps this is because learning objectives are rarely assigned to story time and consequently it is perceived as lacking validity, i.e. if it cannot be tested it loses curriculum time. We do not support the use of prescribed learning objectives for any session in schools. It follows, that a good read-aloud session will not have specific objectives either, the only aim is for children to experience what books have to offer. The text is presented as a whole. It is not cut into separate levels of language (sentence, word of text) by the teacher, but instead children are given an example of what words can do in the form of rich narratives. The teacher who reads the story adds to her professional repertoire of roles during story time. She models the full potential of being a reader. She dynamically opens the door to the world of texts and their rich meanings for experienced or inexperienced readers, enticing them to be like her and do what she does – enjoying the exciting and emotional world of books.

We know that read-aloud times offer a range of experiences about the process of reading (Hughes 1970; Britton 1982; Taylor 1994), but they also provide opportunities for children to learn about language features and the organisational aspects of the text, importantly in the context of a whole story (Perera 1984; Hansen 1987).Within this environment, the experience of reading is made visible and tangible for early readers. Chambers (1991) writes that: 'We cannot easily read for ourselves what we haven't heard said. We learn to read by joining in with those who know how to do it, gradually taking it on ourselves' (p. 51). Chambers compares reading aloud to children to what Vygotsky (1978) would call 'a loaning of consciousness'. The teacher creates a 'zone of proximal development' by engaging in an activity that the children are unable to undertake on their own at that moment in their learning. The children are inducted into an activity that the culture considers rich in reward. The teacher's role is of master or mistress of the apprentices. Like Hans Sachs in Wagner's opera *Meistersinger* who, in his work shop in Nuremburg, teaches his student singers in the art of composition and performance of song, teachers of literacy demonstrate the way the tunes and patterns of language can be released from the page by reading.

Hearing stories read from an early age demonstrates how the writing found in books 'works'. Listening to books read aloud is a preparation for when children go on to do it themselves. It provides 'pointers' to what children will find and what they should look out for when they begin to perform the more challenging task of doing it for themselves (Chambers 1991). Children can relax while hearing the teacher read, as the onus is given to the reader to decode the text, hold the listeners' attention and allow the words to do their task inside the heads of those who listen.

For early readers, hearing books read presents the magic of turning marks on the page into events, people, worlds and encounters that can frighten, amuse and thrill. In doing so, the listeners of stories can experience together how these written marks, brought to life by reading, can invoke a gamut of emotions. This really is like magic, as the words read produce pictures in minds and can show children a means of psychological escape from the primary world of everyday consciousness into a new form of cognitive being. Communally, a story time offers a consciousness that children recognise – it is the world of imaginative play, but assisted this time by authors who know how to entice children in. Drawing on Vygotsky (1978) again, experiencing books read within a social context will be gradually internalised by the children so that they can form the psychological mechanisms required to 'read to themselves'.

Children hearing books together offers a model of participation in the way the children are invited to make meanings together. Read-aloud times honour children's capacity to learn about reading within these relatively informal social contexts and highlights their ability to participate in enjoying stories and poems from an early age. If story times become a regular feature of community classroom life, and a culture of enjoying a range of texts authored by people whose only aim is to challenge and entertain the young is fostered, then books become fundamentally important emotionally and intellectually as another way of understanding the world. In story times, children and teachers genuinely enjoy the emotional and intellectual affordances of literature – not primarily as teachers and pupils in institutions but as human beings in a cultural community.

Reading aloud and the teaching of phonics

Many of the best children's books make great use of rhyme to make the stories memorable and to provide extra cues for those children who are beginning to learn to read (Barrs and Thomas 1991). Rhymes also direct children's attention to the shapes and sounds of words and how sounds are written. As already discussed in this book, research over twenty years ago (Bryant and Bradley 1985) showed that children's knowledge of nursery rhymes was an indication of their potential to learn to read. Children who listen to rhymes of all kinds develop phonological awareness and sensitivity to sounds and the features of words. Rhyming language, by its very nature, draws attention to itself (Barrs and Thomas 1991) and children love to hear how authors play games with the sounds that words make. Children's authors exploit the use of patterns in rhyme and the beginnings and endings of words take on dynamic significance in the games that are played within the text. Initial letters may be used for alliteration and word-endings make the rhymes. Children experience and learn about phonology within the contexts of happy and noisy chanting and singing of the words along with the characters in the books and other children in the class. There will be children who learn to read independently through hearing books read and then joining in. They learn all they need to about phonology by this method and, with the help of semantic and syntactic strategies, go on to be independent readers.

Box 7.1

- Look again at how often you have a read-aloud time: plan story time spots in the week – in the morning, before lunch, before independent reading to whet appetites, before home time. In planning meetings with colleagues, encourage them to do the same.
- If you feel you need to, practise reading the books at home to family and friends or to yourself. Try out 'silly' voices; find out what's going to happen in the book before the children.
- Get the school to subscribe to a children's literature magazine like *Books for Keeps* (www.booksforkeeps.co.uk/) or go to the *Write Away* web site (www.writeaway.org.uk/) to learn about new books coming out that may interest your class.
- Try the three-book approach – in one sitting, read a short picture book that the children know well, then one that the children are beginning to know and finally one that is unknown. Encourage the children to sing or join in with the lines.
- Swap classes with a colleague to read stories that you love to read – your enthusiasm for books will spread to the children.
- Keep a record of the books that you have read – this will ensure that your reading aloud programme has coherence and continuity.
- Ask the children to start a reading journal for their journey through the book being read. Do some pre-reading activities – prediction from the cover and the blurb for example. As you read, ask the children to record new characters who come into the story and at the end of the reading-aloud time ask them to respond to what has been read – ask them to make pencil illustrations of characters and events that occur.
- Ask the children to respond to the content of read-aloud sessions by freeze-framing the meaning and events of the pages or chapters – For example, freeze-frame Chapter 1 by going into role as the characters in pairs at moments of tension between them. Or, at points where decisions have to be made by characters, construct a 'decision alley' – line the children up facing each other to form a tunnel or alley. One side of the line will give you one option to take, the other side will provide reasons to take the other option. Walk through as the character as the children in the lines whisper to you.

Independent reading times

Do you 'Drop Everything and Read' (DEAR) in your class? Have you had USSR (Uninterrupted Sustained Silent Reading) recently? Maybe it is time you had a SQUIRT (Sustained Quiet Uninterrupted Independent Reading Time). Whichever form of reading time is utilised in the classroom, children need to read different reading materials for their own purposes (Hall and Coles 1999). Classrooms that always impose the types of reading that children should experience do not develop independence or contribute to readers' control or motivation (Grainger and Tod 2000). Children must feel they have choice and agency about their reading lives.

   Children can be encouraged to recognise the validity of reading at one's own pace and with reading material that the children have chosen them-selves to satisfy their own emotional and intellectual needs. Teachers cannot always know what the children will enjoy. Equally, the teacher may not always need to be involved in responses to the texts available in the class-room. It is not possible to know the emotional and intellectual backgrounds that children bring to stories that form their responses. Space can be pro-vided for the children to form their own meanings and emotional and intel-lectual reactions. Independent reading time offers all these opportunities and provides a time for children to participate by making their own reading choices and allowing them to practise finding the pleasures in a variety of reading materials. Independent reading also can show children that reading is something that does not always or only happen when one is alone. Reading can be a social time. It is an activity that can happen alongside other people and it is possible to share the experience of reading good books, magazines, comics and poems together. Margaret Meek (1991) has written that she knows reading to be

> a fully social activity, shared with my family, students, children in school and those who have read more than I ever shall. In engaging with others' reading I discover more of what is in the text: I add their meanings to mine. Together we explore what written language, in all its forms, is like. (p. 41)

Learning about phonics independently

Judging by the documentation from governments about how to teach pho-nics, one might only conceive of children learning grapho-phonic strategies and knowledge about phonology directly from the teacher. This is not true (Goodman 1993). Activities that develop young children's knowledge about letters and sounds need to build on what children already know. As we have already discussed, children's phonological development happens in a range of ways that might be out of sight and hearing of teachers. For example, they skip and sing and make up playground rhymes, all of which contribute to their understanding of the sounds of language. Their participation in learning more about these things is essential. Fortunately, children are very curious about written language. Making independent reading part of the reading routines contributes to a classroom environment that honours their ability to learn independently.

Independent reading times provide the opportunity to practise reading and to try out the developing skills and strategies children are using. Allowing children to start to recognise words within contexts for themselves or supported by their peers in reading partners, sharing books in a social and friendly environment, is a very powerful way of building up a reading culture in classrooms that can nurture all the skills children need to learn to read. The children will revisit books that have been made familiar by the teacher or through repeated reading with their friends. By doing so, they develop a core of texts they know well and will reinforce their understanding of the strategies they need to use to read the text. Seeing others using letter-to-sound correspondence and other important strategies to read will bolster confidence in developing readers.

Box 7.2

- Make independent reading time happen every day. By the age of seven, children should have at least 15 minutes a session. You may have two sessions a day (Chambers 1991).
- Make your reading times varied and dynamic. Make each day different in some way – for example, Mondays are for reading partners; Tuesdays are poetry only; Wednesdays are quiet reading days; Thursdays are book-type tables – when types of book such as fairy tales, non-fiction, comics, poetry, etc. are all given a separate table and children choose where they want to sit; Fridays are non-fiction days.
- Organise reading partners for certain days – the best partnerships are those chosen by the children themselves.
- Create a system of book buddies across the age ranges so that older children go and read to younger children.
- Have recorded stories available with multiple headsets – record yourself telling the stories the children love.
- Brings your own book in and read alongside the children.
- Read a section from a story or a poem to whet the children's appetite for independent reading time before it begins.
- At the end of the session, ask a few children to give a 'juicy bit' from what they have been reading for the rest of the class to enjoy.

(Continued)

(Continued)

- Using Post-it notes, ask the children to write recommendations and stick them in the inside cover for others to discover.
- Create story boxes, which are small boxes with a theme. For example, the seaside story box might have a collection of sea shells, some plastic figures, fish and sea animals. The box is decorated to depict a seaside scene. This encourages playful story-making.

Shared reading

Shared reading involves the joint participation of teachers and children around a shared text. Often the text will be a 'big book' – a large-format story book – which the group read together in a variety of ways. The teacher is able to demonstrate reading with the children as a class and focus upon particular aspects of the processes or strategies of reading. In addition, the teacher can concentrate on particular structures of written genre highlighting the use of particular types of words and sentences that contribute to the meaning of the text. This makes shared reading different to story time, which we have explored earlier. In shared reading, the teacher may have particular aspects of the book or strategies for reading to highlight. S/he may instigate discussions with the children about events or characters within the texts, or may want to focus upon grammar or vocabulary. Story time is all about hearing books read for pleasure and that is all. Shared reading, on the other hand, is an opportunity for explicit teaching but in a collaborative and democratic atmosphere. The books the teacher chooses to use in shared reading will usually be within the range of the children's comprehension level, but often above the independent reading abilities of the majority of the class. This way, challenge is provided and an opportunity to extend the skills that the children already have (Strickland and Morrow 1990; Swindal 1993). Everything the teacher does with the book in front of the children is there to demonstrate what happens while we read. Through her actions, the teacher makes explicit the thoughts, processes and skills that are engaged during a reading.

Shared reading offers opportunities to introduce to children everything we need to teach about reading. These are the **processes** and **skills** of reading. Shared reading times can be set up to demonstrate the processes of reading – asking children to discuss and compare their personal experiences of these processes:

- *Predicting* – exploring what the text provides for its readers to hypothesise what will come next – this will include the pictures inside and outside the book.
- *Picturing* – describing the internal 'pictures' the group 'see' in their heads when the book is read.

- *Connecting* – exploring everyone in the shared reading group's personal connection with the characters and events in the story. Have the children seen or heard anything similar in their lives? What do the characters and events remind them of?
- *Questioning* – encouraging the children to interrogate the text. The children are encouraged to ask questions of the characters and events of the story.
- *Engaging* – the teacher demonstrates emotional and intellectual engagement with the story. It is important to explore through discussion what the story makes us feel inside.
- *Evaluating* – the teacher and children are given the opportunity in shared reading to cast judgements on the text, which develops the children's confidence to read the text critically. (Grainger and Todd 2000).

Shared reading also enables children to see reading in action and to explore the affordances of reading.

Strategies and skills

- *Semantic cues* – learning to predict the words coming up from the children's own knowledge of the worlds the books depict.
- *Syntactic cues* – showing the children how they can draw on their own implicit understanding of grammar to predict the words coming up.
- *Grapho-phonic cues* – learning the letter/s-to-sound correspondence and how they can be utilised for reading and spelling.

Shared reading provides opportunities to explore the processes and strategies one needs to understand to be fluent readers, while at the same time allowing the enjoyment of whole stories, poems or information texts.

Shared reading and phonics

Children need to learn the strategies to use when they come across an unfamiliar word. They need to know there are a number of successful strategies they can draw on to take meaning off the page. They also need to know that they should not rely too heavily on one strategy. This includes not putting too much emphasis on grapho-phonic strategies as it is frequently unreliable in the English language. Balance and breadth of strategies is essential for children learning the skills they need to read fluently. As we have already explained in this book, there is little evidence to even suggest that all children need to learn through a single strategy like synthetic phonics. The English language and the people who learn it are too complex and varied to be offered any kind of thin gruel (Meek 1991) of reading experience. Shared reading enables the teacher to demonstrate all the reading strategies that Goodman (1967) described – semantic, syntactic and grapho-phonic (see Chapter 2) – and allow the children to discover them and their affordances themselves. Shared reading can offer the opportunities to learn all these strategies alongside the main focus which will always be the construction of meanings and the ensuing delight and rapture they bring.

Shared reading can be used to draw children's attention to the detail of the print. From the age of three upwards, many children will be able to take an interest in the shapes and structures of words and be aware of similarities between them (Dombey and Moustafa 1998). Teachers can draw children's attention to syllables in the words that are well known to them and how words can be broken down into smaller units. Asking children to clap the syllabic make-up of words, for example, is fun and perfect for shared reading times. This will emphasise the rhythmic patterns of words, phrases and rhymes. It is important to emphasise that none of this needs be done outside the context of rich meaning-making that accompanies the use of good books and poems.

We know that children respond well to 'onset' and 'rime' (Goswami 2002) (see Chapter 2), so using poetry and rhymes again and again will draw children's attention to these patterns in the texts. Furthermore, the children may wish to collect groupings of words from the stories and poems they encounter to sort into sets according to initial letters or pairs of letters or by the way the rhyme ends. These activities, completed in the rich and satisfying context of reading real books, will encourage an interest in words and their structures. The activities add to a culture in early years classrooms, reflecting a love of language and how it works to make meanings.

The use of alphabet books in shared reading also offers a rich and enjoyable way of drawing children's attention to print and how words are structured. Simply linking the first letters of the children's names to the appropriate page in the book allows children to feel confident about letter–sound relationships.

Box 7.3

- Use drama techniques to draw out the rich meanings within the text, e.g. freeze-frames that depict the main events, improvisations for the consequences of the characters and the events in the story. Do not be afraid to stop the reading suddenly and 'snap into drama'.
- Ask groups of children to read sections of the text together – perhaps the voices of particular characters.
- Emphasise punctuation by asking the class to make a sound for each punctuation mark as you read a great book. They then use their agreed sounds when the story is read.
- Ask the children to get into 'beat teams'. They can be one, two or three beat teams. The children need to sort words from a text the teacher is reading to create a list.

- Play a cloze-procedure game. Cover up words with Post-it notes. Ask the children to speculate what the words could be from and the evidence they are given from the rest of the text and the pictures. In pairs, ask them to write down what they think the word is on a whiteboard. When the word is revealed, ask the children which strategies they used to find the word. If the children predict words that are not completely accurate but do not change the meaning, take them as being correct.

Guided reading and one-to-one

Guided reading and one-to-one reading both offer the perfect opportunity for teachers to work with children who have particular needs. It is a time for micro-teaching – 'chamber pedagogy'. These groupings allow teachers to concentrate on these needs, whatever they may be. Teachers might find it useful to work with disaffected readers, quiet girls/boys, children who need their attention drawn to the print, those who require learning how to draw on semantic or syntactic strategies, children who are more experienced readers and would benefit from more discussion of characterisation or other aspects of response. Both guided reading and one-to-one enable teachers to tailor their guidance to the needs of the group or individual. They also offer a useful time for assessment of the children's development within a supportive atmosphere. Guided reading is when the teacher leads the learning among a small group of children. This may be any number of children from two up to four or five. One-to-one teaching is when the teacher works with one child only.

In most cases guided reading and one-to-one is centred on a whole text – a book or a poem. The teacher is there to mediate the children's introduction to the text according to the needs of the specific children in the group or one-to-one. In most cases, the children will be provided with their own copy of the text. The teacher will often introduce the text, perhaps asking the children to predict and hypothesise about its content. All the time, the approach is tailored to the needs of those children in the group or the individual one-to-one. These moments provide ideal opportunities for the teacher to utilise data from miscue and running records and concentrate on the strategies the children need to learn to become fluent readers. This form of organisation is a genuine attempt to introduce 'personal learning' and is a far richer, effective and nuanced form of teaching than the vulgar 'scattergun' approach offered by those who propose a whole-class teaching of synthetic phonics for all children whether they need it or not. The efficacy and approach to guided reading and one-to-one sessions honours the individual experiences and development of children. It enables careful 'chamber pedagogy' to be developed and fine-tuned for the individuals in the group or the one-to-one. This is real detailed teaching that draws on the knowledge the teacher has of the individuals in the class.

The groups are often not static. Children may be in a variety of different small-group sessions for a variety of reasons. Teachers may wish to organise mixed-experienced groups within which children are encouraged to assist each other. Teachers often avoid static groupings to dispel or discourage developing cultures and identities based around achievement or underachievement. This way, children perceive the groups as being a pedagogy that is fine-tuned to assist everyone's development in different ways and can change depending on what is being explored or read at the time.

Many of the ideas and activities with whole texts teachers may use with shared reading can be applied with a smaller focused group. However, for those children who need to have their attention focused on the print, the box below provides some examples of ideas that can be used to develop their analytic ability and knowledge of letters and sounds.

Box 7.4

- While reading and talking about a whole text that the teacher or the children are reading in the group, draw attention to the features of words that are like other words the children know already. The children can be encouraged to make analogies between the words they know and ones that are new to them.
- Using rhyming texts, teachers can help the children break words down into onsets and rimes (see Chapter 2) so that they can read and write new words by analogy with the words they know.
- Small-group and one-to-one work provides the perfect opportunity to make class alphabet books linked to class interests or topics. These books can utilise children's knowledge of popular culture.
- Play games with words and letters like 'I spy' Use rimes to help them find the object in the room that is being thought of by the teacher – 'I spy with my little eye some thing ending in "ate"'.
- Use nonsense poetry to discuss with the children how we are able to read nonsense words. The children could make a nonsense dictionary.
- Using an interesting book drawn from the class collection of real books, the teacher can demonstrate the use of grapho-phonic cues in reading. The teacher could show that using the initial sounds, looking at word endings and breaking the words into parts can be useful strategies to use to help read unfamiliar words.
- When children are reading in guided groups or one-to-one, the teacher can explicitly ask the children to explain how they knew how to read a word. A general discussion can begin over the different strategies that can be used when reading unfamiliar words.
- Guided and one-to-one sessions provide the teacher with the opportunity talk to children about their reading – what they like and what they do not like about reading, who they like to read with, where they like to read and so on. Knowing the children's likes and dislikes about reading will assist the teacher to plan reading sessions in the future and also allows the teacher and child to get to know each other in a friendly and supportive way.

All the ideas provided in box 7.4 would be used when the teacher has assessed the children's development in terms of their developing knowledge of the processes and strategies needed for reading. Most children will not need direct teaching of phonics, as they may be fluent readers already or may be on the path to becoming fluent readers without the need for phonics instruction. These chamber-teaching sessions enable children to work closely with a supportive experienced reader who has apprenticed these children in the processes and skills of reading.

Learning to read can be a joy if a safe and supportive environment is created for the learners and the teachers. The routines of reading are intrinsic to creating reading cultures in the classroom. As long as variety, interesting texts and consistent enthusiasm for meaning-making from the more experienced adults are present, then children will see these routines as a warm and reassuring opportunity to develop as readers. Research (Medwell et al. 1999) has shown that the most effective teachers of literacy are those teachers who privilege meaning-making in their teaching of reading and who embed their teaching of the skills of reading within whole-text activities. The routines of reading that we have described in this chapter all privilege the creation of meaning by demonstrating and modelling how reading can happen and what it can do.

Conclusion

This chapter has provided ideas for establishing routines for the teaching of reading and the learning of phonics. Routines make up the way a school day is passed and provide the substance of a rich reading culture. Routines offer some predictability, but at the same time they do not offer boredom. Routines are not all provided in the same way. On the contrary, teachers will be ensuring that routines offer a rich variety of activities that are enthusiastically offered by practitioners determined to provide excitement and intrigue.

Further reading

King, C. and Briggs, J. (2005) *Literature Circles*. Royston: UK Literacy Association.
Rogoff, B. (2003) *The Cultural Nature of Human Development*. Oxford: Oxford University Press.

Talk, reading and writing

In this chapter we aim:

- to show how talk, reading and writing are interconnected in children's early lives and this should be reflected in the classroom;
- to describe ways of engaging children in books and stories through play – drama and role play should be carefully crafted and frequently provided;
- to propose that independent writing opportunities for functional and imaginative purposes should be found and children's endeavours celebrated;
- to signify that affective engagements with texts are the key to success;
- to emphasise that children's self-esteem should be nurtured and preserved in the teaching and learning of literacy.

Previously the importance of the connection between reading, writing and speaking and listening has been mentioned. In this chapter we will discuss the ways that the links are formed and promote activities to draw together children's learning in these three modes. Earlier, we described children living and growing in a print-full environment. So too are children surrounded by voices and sounds from before their birth as they 'tune in' to the sounds and patterns of their mother's voice and on into babyhood and then childhood. And this is where the roots of literacy are to be found. Early sounds become symbolic for babies and young children and their cries, their early voices, are also representative of how they feel (Winnicott 1964). In fact we know that babies become very quickly attuned to the sounds of their environment, which is obviously culturally framed. In the early months of life we now know that 'just as facial discrimination is determined by the faces present in a baby's natural environment, so sound discrimination is determined by the sounds in a baby's environment' (Blakemore and Frith 2005: 38). So, as well as the sounds and patterns of the voice they heard before they were born, babies are tuning into and discriminating between individual sounds around them during the first year of their life. Further, Blakemore and Frith report that at three to four months of age 'the brain already seems to be geared up to process language' (p. 39). The suggestion here is that these early experiences of sound and language are shaping the brain and inevitably the shape forms mirrors the culture of their early environment. While the brain is wired to process language, the kind of language it processes is dependent on what is around them.

> Well before babies are able to utter any recognisable words, they start to babble. From about seven months, babies produce all sorts of sounds, such as 'bababa' and 'dadada', and noises, such as clicks and gurgles. Not all of these will later be part of their native speech. But babbling often includes sounds that make up the language in the babies' environment. It seems plausible that this is a useful mechanism to learn how to produce the sounds of one's language. On the other hand, even children who hardly babble at all still learn to speak. Thus learning to speak may go on without any external signs of practice. (Blakemore and Frith 2005: 43)

This sensitivity to sounds is often supported by the use of 'motherese' by adults around the babies and continues with most, though not all, children experiencing the comforting sounds of songs, lullabies and nursery rhymes. These serve functions other than comfort for the developing child. Already they are helping children in their growing phonological awareness, as they develop an ear for patterns in language. As children are invited to play along with language, contributing to end rhymes, for example *Jack and Jill went up the* ..., they are learning some important lessons about rhythm, onset and rime – which will all contribute seriously to their later development as readers and writers. Alliteration also plays a part in this, for example 'Peter Piper Pecked a Piece of Pickled Pepper' and other tongue twisters, or 'Sing a Song of Sixpence', where children's attention is drawn towards the repeated initial sound. During these kinds of activities parents and other family members 'apply oral markers, such as stress and intonation, to denote syntactic forms' (Corden 2000: 147), additionally contributing to children's language awareness which in turn will help them to read and write.

Box 8.1 Children's knowledge about sounds and language can be developed by encouraging:

- Early knowledge of nursery rhymes
- Awareness of rhyme and alliteration
- The invention of rhymes and alliterative words
- Awareness of the beginning sounds of words (onsets)
- Awareness of the end sounds of words (rimes)

(Whitehead 2009: 46)

What is most important to remember when considering children's early development as language users is that babies and young children are not coerced into talking, listening and playing with language. Rather they are inducted into language practices and learn through the complex processes of imitation and the formation of hypotheses. Fortunately, most children do not undertake this journey alone but in the company of supportive adults and family members. However, 'children learn language because they are predisposed to do so ... children have to work out the way in which language is organised for themselves' (Wells 1986: 81). While most children are supported in these endeavours, children in these early stages are problem-solvers and risk-takers in their language use and these exploratory stages are essential for them in their development. Wells describes children as 'seekers after meaning who try to find the underlying principles that will account for the patterns that they recognise in their experiences' (1986: 43). We believe that in the right school environment children's practices as apprentice language users and 'seekers after meaning' continue to flourish in this way to feed their knowledge of and about language. As well as language play, everyday conversation has a central role to play in language learning, thought and the skills of communication (Vygotsky 1986; Wells 1986; Clay 1998; Corden 2000), with Wells claiming that in order to learn to talk, children need experience of conversation, and that 'quantity is important' (Wells 1986: 44). What is being claimed here is that children are learning about distinct sounds, rhymes, the onset and rimes in words and patterns of language from communities and cultures, and learning to hypothesise about their language, its grammars and meanings, all before school and all in informal contexts as part of everyday living. Their brains are being shaped by the experiences and encounters in their early lives and the areas of the brain associated with learning spoken language and learning to read are being formed. Strong claims are now made for the kinds of early, volitional learning that occurs in the safety and informality of home contexts:

> Research suggests that pre-5s who have had considerable informal experience of sharing rhymes, songs, alphabets, picture books and daily routine talk with carers are already sensitised to language and literacy and likely to make an early start on reading. (Whitehead 2009: 26)

The bridge between this kind of learning and school literacy learning could be small and securely supported if teachers are informed and are ready to acknowledge, celebrate and extend such opportunities. In addition, we know that most children have a spoken vocabulary of more than 2,000 words by the age of five and are ready to continue at this pace of learning in the primary years at school (Blakemore and Frith 2005: 43).

Box 8.2   In Foundation and Key Stage 1 classrooms:

- Teach children nursery rhymes.
- Encourage them to teach each other favourite rhymes from home.
- Play games with nursery rhymes, adapting them, for example 'Jack and Jane went …'
- Create anthologies of rhymes.
- Celebrate playground rhymes, clapping rhymes, skipping rhymes, dipping rhymes …
- Create video or audio tapes of children rhyming.
- Encourage children to create written versions.
- Collect rhymes from parents, grandparents and other community members.

Talk into reading

Children's early talk experiences then are crucial in familiarising them with the rhythms, patterns and sounds in language, helping them to understand the appropriate forms of language, supporting them in realising purposes for language and generally inducting them into language practices. Importantly, rich early experiences help children to take ownership of their language, giving them permission to play, take risks and experiment with words, sounds and meanings. The kind of play with language that occurs informally at home before and outside of school seems to be serving two main functions. First, it is giving children a sense of ownership of their language, providing lessons about how language can be employed for their uses and that it is a valuable tool in families and in society to make things happen, to effect change. Secondly it is attuning children to sounds and patterns in their home language, familiarising them with how language sounds in use, how connections between sounds can be made, like for like, what sounds the same as …, and allows opportunities for children to delight in sounds and patterns as well as make the analogous connections that will become so important to them in their developing skills of reading and writing. The kinds of engaging and trusting environments in which these very important lessons are being learned are special to homes and family contexts but can with care be extended into early years and primary school settings too. Talk contexts, many and varied, need to be created in order for these special learning environments to be successful in school.

Delight in language is then easily extended into playful experiences with print versions of language use in books of stories, poems and rhymes. These experiences need to be noisy, that is, language at this stage needs to be heard to be appreciated and the sounds of print need to echo in the ears of young developing readers. It is of great importance that these early school encounters with print literacy are informal and enjoyable, enticing children into the joy that can be found in books rather than creating any anxiety. At these early stages there will not be a 'one size fits all' template for children as they will arrive from a range of different experiences and encounters with language use and with print. However, it is at this point that affective pedagogies earn their place in schools as the potential to disaffect children in relation to 'school reading' is very high in the early years. What we know is that children's early delight in the sounds of language needs to be sensitively harnessed to extend into a delight in the rewards from print language. Feeling the sounds of words on their lips, identifying how that looks on the page and sharing the reading of the text is a huge stride across the bridge from the intimacy and play with books at home towards school literacy practices.

Box 8.3   In Foundation, Key Stage and Key Stage 2 classrooms:

- Read aloud frequently to children to immerse them in the sounds of language from books and stories.
- Include a repertoire of books with patterned and predictable language, e.g. *We're going on a Bear Hunt; Each Peach Pear Plum; The Train Ride; Brown Bear, Brown Bear; Where's My Teddy?; Room on the Broom; Whiff, The Fish who Could Wish; Giraffes Can't Dance ...*
- Record these stories so that children can hear them spoken as well as using the book to identify print (perhaps ask parents, grandparents, other family members to make the tapes).
- Record the children reading these stories.
- Make opportunities for children to share the books, with each other, with adults in school, with parent/grandparent volunteers ...
- Make class versions in big book style.
- Create class displays of refrains from favourite books.
- Use these books in shared and guided reading sessions to model the sounds of print and to help children identify familiar print.

Playing with print can extend beyond developing visual familiarity with printed texts. We know that children's engagement with books, stories and reading across the curriculum can be secured through other kinds of 'play' with texts – role play, drama and storytelling – which all engage children in developing a multi-sensory awareness of language as they develop reading competence. There are, however, finely tuned pedagogical decisions to be made here. There is a danger always that talk opportunities in school are simply appropriated for 'agendarised', curriculum-driven tasks. That is, children's authentic and so highly-motivated purposes for talk are often subjugated to rather more spurious inauthentic or contrived reasons that meet targets or produce outcomes to help teachers to meet their targets. We know, however, the joy to be found in sharing talk for personal purposes, for its intrinsic worth rather than for any added value to achieving externally set targets or preset outcomes. Further to this argument, we know that play and language can be similarly thought of. As Whitehead describes:

> Language and play share several characteristics: both use symbols to stand for a range of ideas, feelings and experiences, both are reflections of human thinking and also creators of new thoughts; both are part of our genetic make up. (Whitehead 2009: 23)

Given this understanding it is incumbent upon teachers to find ways to ensure that children's own talk is given opportunities to flourish, is valued and celebrated, as well as the kind of talk that is often found, a kind of lip-service to valuing talk, using talk to serve curriculum purposes rather than children's purposes. Of course this also opens up discussions of power and language in relation to classroom discourses but valuing children's talk serves real purposes for teachers too. With the knowledge that language is 'the tool of all person-made tools' (Hall 2004: 89) which helps us by providing shape to our developing thoughts and understandings but also, in this process, is responsible for shaping our brains, our pedagogy must be influenced. From the work of neuroscience we now know that the brain's plasticity allows its connectivity to be reviewed, renewed and changed and that experience, including conversation, is responsible for these changes (Greenfield 2000). As Blakemore and Frith (2005) remind us not only does 'education change minds' but education also changes brains. Of course, research work carried out a century ago had already concluded that 'thought development is defined by language' (Vygotsky 1986: 94) but highly relevant to this book's messages about how children learn to read is Vygotsky's additional claim that:

> Systematicity and consciousness do not come from outside, displacing the child's spontaneous concepts, but that on the contrary, they presuppose the existence of rich and relatively mature representations. (Vygotsky 1986: 172)

Vygotsky is describing the way that reciprocity works in educational contexts and in doing so is dismissing the notion that new learning (scientific concepts) can be imposed but instead must take its place in making connections with existing learning. He also rejects the notion that education can be seen 'as a kind of superstructure erected over maturation' or that education can be seen to be 'related to development as consumption to production' (p. 175), and we now know from close studies of how our brains actually develop that his theories can be supported. Teaching and learning frequently occupy different rhythms, one does not presuppose the other and there can be no 'one size fits all' without mistakenly assuming that all children have had identical early experiences. If we now draw this argument toward reading development it is possible to see that language and literacy encounters before and outside of school will influence new learning opportunities in school, and further that talk offers both a mirror in which children's knowledge and understanding is reflected as well as a vehicle for new understandings to develop. Structured talk opportunities then through the use of drama and role play and through frequent storytelling contexts are both necessary and illuminating in classroom contexts.

Box 8.4

- Plan for talk to occur regularly and frequently in class time.
- Ensure that sometimes this talk is for children's own purposes or at least enable them to have an element of choice and control over the content, form, structure and purpose for talk.
- As well as talking about books and stories – book gossip – make opportunities for children to share talk with a range of audiences and talk partners.
- Carefully listen to children talking.
- Monitor children's developing abilities to use, imitate and repeat sounds, rhymes and patterns in language.
- Construct opportunities for children to make conversation, perhaps with children they are not usually working with.
- Create times for children to develop their story telling, conversational, anecdotal and responsive talk skills.
- Actively encourage talk while children are playing alone or with others.

Drama, role play, reading and writing

Young children, in their early encounters with books and stories, will naturally use movement, gesture and 'voices' to engage with texts. Children, either on their own or in the company of parents, siblings or other family members, are often seen playing their way through texts, interweaving their own understandings and existing knowledge into the fictive world. Such play involves young children in employing all of their senses and connecting texts with other experiences. These kinds of encounters with meaning through playing with books pave the way for meaningful encounters with print. If, as we argue, print is simply a vehicle for meaning and so constructing meaning is the first and only aim for readers, then using a range of strategies to model, encourage and enable children to draw meaning from texts will lead them towards employing print in order to serve their purpose. As Adams maintains, 'If we want children to learn to read well, we must find a way to induce them to read lots' (Adams 1990: 5). One way of achieving this, as discussed in other chapters, is through the use of play, including role play and drama. Playing their way into stories, using stories as the foundation for their play, playing with ideas from the stories and with characters are all natural occurrences as children need to continually make links with prior and other learning in order to make sense of their lives. While this may happen incidentally, often out of our sight and range, it is also important for teachers to plan for this kind of opportunity to occur inside classrooms so that they can ensure that it occurs for the benefit of all children and also to enable them to monitor children's engagement with stories. More formally perhaps, drama conventions may be more carefully controlled and structured, but will still provide ways for children to emotionally engage with literature and stories generally and to personally construct themselves inside texts as 'they inhabit a fictional world and respond to the conflicts and tensions experienced in it ... Generating ideas, expressing and constructing meaning in a variety of ways and reflecting upon their insights' (Grainger et al. 2005: 118). Additionally, through drama, children are able to view and hear the responses of other children to literature and to stories read and told and in that way their own repertoire of voice can be extended (Grainger et al. 2005; Barrs and Cork 2001). Drama, storytelling and role play also provide reasons for writing as children are invited to use their own written script to join in with the story, extend it and personalise it through a range of strategies designed to help children to make sense themselves of the texts they are being introduced to. While, for example, drawing and annotating a map to help a story character to escape from the clutches of a wicked witch, a pirate or an enraged dragon ..., or writing a list of instructions for the Three Billy Goats Gruff to cross the bridge safely away from the troll, or writing a shopping list of food to take to the dragon's cave or to their treasure island, children are deeply engaged with the content of the story but also learning the skills of authoring as well as employing print for seemingly authentic purposes. This kind of enjoyable and engaging activity extends children's meetings with print and helps them to explore both meanings of stories as well as the ways in which they can be expressed. Of course, teachers need to be knowledgeable, as described in an earlier chapter, to take advantage of the creative practices that really help children to learn about the uses of print in these ways.

Box 8.5

- Invent drama opportunities from read and told stories.
- Use drama to draw together talk, reading and writing opportunities.
- Craft opportunities for children to write in role during drama to help them feel the power of writing to influence action and behaviour.
- Encourage role play both as an independent part of children's own play and also by shaping opportunities for children to take on a role from a story in a structured drama activity.

(Continued)

(Continued)

- Find creative opportunities for children to write about characters in stories, as those characters in stories themselves or in response to characters in stories.
- Make connections between traditional tales and drama.
- In plans, include opportunities for children to frequently 'inhabit' stories and there to make use of print responses and print engagement.
- Ensure that children have constant opportunities to collaborate with others, through drama, role play and their own play in order to contribute to and learn from the engagement of others.

Once children have learned that print can be useful to manage the behaviour of others, and if they have a sense of ownership of the print landscape in their classroom, then writing, for example, open and closed signs for shops and cafes in the role-play area, writing directions to the next village, directing others to the birds they can see from their classroom windows, writing warning signs next to their models of monsters, making notices for visitors, making maps, drawing stories – all become part of their everyday lives as they learn to feel empowered by print. In the early years, when children are inexperienced writers, these kinds of signs, notices and useful environmental print messages may take the form of mark-making before they have learned to conform to conventional alphabetic print, or it make take the form of letters of their own name repeated and rearranged in different orders to represent meaning. The important aspect of this kind of activity, however, is that children are learning to take control of print, fearlessly, in the knowledge that teachers and other adults surrounding them will enjoy and take notice of their writing, help them when they need help, guide them in respect of resources as well as alphabetic knowledge and, most importantly, celebrate their writing and print knowledge. Of course these kinds of early writing examples are also invaluable for teachers' formative assessments as they loudly demonstrate what it is that children already know about phonology, phonemes, 'their growing mastery of orthography' (Adams 1990: 430) and the forms and functions of language. Writing in these early stages should not be seen as a separate activity to reading but closely interconnected as children learn to employ and manipulate print as they inhabit stories as described above, use print to effect action, write their own and others' names frequently and for real purposes, and persuade adults to read and make meaning from their early writing/mark-making endeavours. We cannot overemphasise the importance of encouraging this kind of independent writing in classrooms which should occur every day and the close, nurturing support it requires to help to sustain it and the growing self-esteem of young emerging writers.

Box 8.6

- Ensure that children feel safe to write, to take risks in their writing.
- Provide opportunities for children to write for real purposes and for real audiences:

  - in response to stories
  - about stories
  - extending stories
  - from inside stories
  - authoring their own stories
  - for functional reasons, for example to name and claim ownership, to warn, to inform, to engage others, to instruct …

- Give children reasons to collaborate and allow collaborations frequently and for children's purposes as well as those of teachers.
- Provide a range of writing resources that invite children's use.
- Ensure that writing resources are freely available to children for their own purposes.
- Include paper, card and pre-made books that will suggest purpose and audience to children.
- Allow children to use the classroom environment for their own print purposes, inviting children to make notices and signs and contribute to displays.
- Celebrate children's mark-making and early writing.
- Monitor children's use of print and attitudes to writing.
- Monitor the connections children make between printed stories and texts and their own emergent writing.

Conclusion

Earlier we noted how Chambers had discovered that the single most influential factor in his own reading development was the opportunity to talk about books – and listen to others talk about books they had read – in an encouraging, affective, conversational environment (Chambers 1993). We would like to extend this idea and claim that children are influenced in their use of print and their understanding of print through opportunities to talk, play, write and read as often as possible in the company of genuinely supportive adults and other children. We would urge teachers to make classrooms safe environments for children to fully engage during these activities as they explore voices represented in books and stories and find and extend their own voice through active engagement in a range of ways, with a range of texts and with a varying range of people. We also ask that children have frequent independent opportunities to read, write and play as well as more structured activities designed for their support.

In this chapter we argue for authenticity to have a key place in the early years experiences at school, to reflect children's home experiences and to build on these, demonstrating the functions and forms of written language and the place that a sense of audience plays in written texts. We also claim that children's own sense of place in classrooms, that is their feelings of ownership of the environment, resources and opportunities to use print, make a difference to whether or not children will affectively engage with literacy events. Combined with this is the very real issue that how children feel about their abilities to use print and read print contributes significantly to their success as readers and writers. Developing and maintaining children's self-esteem is of prime concern.

Further reading

Chambers, A. (1993) *Tell Me: Children Reading and Talk*. Stroud: Thimble Press.
Corden, R. (2000) *Literacy and Understanding Through Talk*. Maidenhead: Open University Press/McGraw-Hill.

9

Assessment of reading

In this chapter we aim:

- to described what information teachers need to collect about their children in order to teach reading;
- to suggest the use of running records as children develop as readers;
- to critically examine frameworks for assessing children's reading development;
- to describe other strategies, including reading conferences, reading diaries and journals and informal methods of assessment.

In this chapter we concentrate on how teachers can assess children's reading development in meaningful ways and in ways that will assist in children's further progress. We begin with a general discussion about assessment for literacy, the different forms it can take and the reasons for doing it in the first place. We want to draw readers' attention to some contemporary methods encouraged by governments and try to explain why these may be more harmful than helpful in the education process. The second section puts forward practical ideas about how to assess children's reading so that teachers reading this book can decide whether they think they would be advantageous for their children in their schools.

Assessment for living

All through this book we have attempted to demonstrate that literacy is not just a set of all-purpose skills and strategies to be learned. Literacy is far more complex, social and personal than that, and learning to be literate also involves developing one's identity, relationships, values and dispositions alongside new skills and strategies (Gee 2001). It is with this in mind that assessment methods need to be studied. We think it is important to remember that education is a social process and that children who are becoming literate and are learning to read are also being taught how to live with others in society (Johnstone and Costello 2009). Assessment is integral to the children's and teachers' learning. It has a very visible place in most schools and can define the forms of relationship that exist between teachers and children and also between legislative bodies and teachers. From this social perspective of learning, the assessment strategies we decide upon must reflect the way we want our society to be and, importantly, the way we wish society to treat people in general. The writers of this book seek a society that is genuinely democratic and caring and which produces people who have strong convictions, are enthusiastic about ideas and activities, but have open and questioning minds and who respect the diverse nature of individuals, communities and their needs (Johnstone and Costello 2009). This understanding of the connection between the social world, education and literacy will make this the first consideration of those devising assessment methods.

How one assesses reading development, as with literacy progress in general, will affect how teaching is organised and practised and how we conceptualise children and childhood (Johnstone 1997; Moss 1998). When assessment is undertaken using high-stakes summative testing and because these tests will affect the lives of the children and the teachers administering them, there is a good deal of evidence to show that the effects can be negative in a variety of ways (Morrison and Joan 2002; Rex and Nelson 2004; Smith 1991; Smith and Rottenberg 1991). First, high-stakes testing, as we have seen in England with Statutory Assessment Tasks (SATs) at the end of Key Stages, restricts the literacy curriculum. This defeats the object of attempts to improve literacy education. Teachers who are under pressure tend to drop the teaching of more complex literacy practices – for example, role play around books and the use of multimedia resources (Rex and Nelson 2004) – as this is deemed to detract from basic and reductive literacy models which can be more easily accessed through written tests. Second, tests like these can have a detrimental impact upon the individual well-being of the teachers in school. High-stakes summative testing has been seen to provoke feelings of outrage from teachers concerning their position and status and this can lead to morale being lowered and feelings of disenchantment (Rex and Nelson 2004). Indeed, it can be argued that the current practices of testing in England and around the developed world are often based on rewarding and punishing children, teachers and school systems. The participants' concentration and focus consequently become shifted towards the number one goal of avoiding punishment or seeking reward by whatever means. This is instead of improving the quality of reading and literacy education (McNeil 2000; Johnstone and Costello 2009). Assessment methods that are based upon testing with high stakes need to be resisted by teachers, and methods which reflect the complex nature of learning to read and write need to be developed.

Assessing pupil progress

In English schools, because of pressure from the government and the local authorities, Assessment of Pupil Progress (APP) is being gradually introduced into schools. This places more emphasis on teacher assessment of the children and may be a move away from testing. APP involves teachers in periodically collecting data on the children and making judgements about their development from a set of criteria (National Strategies 2010). As we write, high-stakes statutory testing is still firmly in place for children at the end of Key Stage 2. Many schools still test children regularly using statutory tests that are optional (in Key Stage 2) or compulsory at the end of a Key Stage. Despite its obvious professional failings, we hope that APP may replace them altogether, but we are not holding our breath!

We would argue that the emphasis in the APP approach is more summative in nature. The materials (National Strategies 2010) contend that APP enables teachers to make 'level judgements' in National Curriculum assessments. Like SATs, they measure children's progress against National Curriculum levels of attainment. Already, one begins to see the reductive nature of this form of assessment. Children's learning development is tied, once again, to arguably narrow and arbitrary National Curriculum levels. So, conceptualisation of children's progress in learning literacy and mathematics is formed for teachers and the profession in APP from narrow government perspectives.

On the APP assessment sheets, descriptors of children's 'performance' in reading are provided for teachers that correspond to National Curriculum levels. These are divided into what the DCSF have called Assessment Foci. For National Curriculum Levels 1 and 2 there is a greater emphasis on the Focus AF1 'Use a range of strategies, including accurate decoding of text, to read for meaning'. Here the descriptors are all primarily concerned with children's ability to use grapho-phonic cues to read texts. There appears to be no real recognition of the validity of children using, for example, picture cues (semantic) to read a text, re-emphasising the government's dogged commitment to teaching phonics to children as their first and potentially only strategy.

Teachers are told in the documentation (DCSF 2009b) that APP is all teachers need to use for assessment of children's literacy. This, I am afraid, is simply not true. It is, instead, an extremely impoverished way of trying to understand children's development. For example, APP takes no interest in what children are choosing to read outside of school. It appears only to take into account what children can do in school. We believe a full reading and literacy assessment must attend to the knowledge and understanding children have about reading: children's confidence and independence, the experience children bring to school, the strategies children are using to read and children's attitudes to reading (Barrs and Thomas 1991). Knowledge of this kind can only be accumulated from observations, conversations with parents and children, and regular 'running records' (discussed below).

Summative and formative assessment

Summative assessments (forms of which we have discussed above) can be seen as the backward-looking assessments (Johnstone and Costello 2009). Tests summarise and judge both the children's attainment and the teacher's success. Formative practice is forward-looking. It will happen during the process of learning and is directed towards affecting future progress (Crooks 1988). The nature of the feedback is of greatest importance. It will often contribute to the positive nature of the process and involve the children in forms of self-assessment, but will not avoid being critical too. Feedback that gives too much praise will lead children to believe that they are always doing well. It has been shown (Dweck 1999) that comments to children that highlight traits such as ability, smartness or goodness can undermine children's ability to foster resilience in their study (Johnstone and Costello 2009). In the next section we suggest ideas on how to assess young children's reading development in ways that we believe reflect education and literacy's place in the social world and honours the subject of teachers' assessment of developing people. The knowledge described below reflects and further emphasises that described earlier in Chapter 3.

Assessing reading

Teachers need to know:

- the knowledge and understanding children have about reading
- children's confidence and independence
- the reading and language experience children have
- the strategies children are using to read
- children's reflection. (Barrs and Thomas 1991)

This knowledge will enable teachers to provide information to children and parents and help plan for the future reading experiences that these children can have in school and even at home.

Knowledge and understanding

Teachers will need to know more about the children's knowledge of books and print. It will be important that children are able to retell stories orally and that when they do so, they use the language of books. It will also be important for the teacher to learn if children notice print when they are out and about on their travels. Children's interest in the letters of their own name or the names of their family is often a sign of their emerging understanding of the use of print around them.

Confidence and independence

When assessing children's confidence and independence it will be important for teachers to discover the contexts within which children are motivated to be readers. Through observations of the children, teachers can study the uses that children make of opportunities that are given to read in classroom routines. It will be important to monitor if children enjoy browsing through books and want to interact with others – play reading, reading with others and their approach to reading with adults. The children's enthusiasm for listening to stories on tape and reading alone will also help the teacher form a view of their confidence and independence. In addition, any difficulties in reading seen in children working across the curriculum will need to be considered. Any sight or hearing difficulties could be discussed with parents informally or in consultation times.

Experience

As we have discussed in previous chapters literacy is associated with cultural environments and consequently the way written and spoken language is used varies. Children's experiences at home and at school will be crucial to understand to help the teacher plan experiences that will be motivating and purposeful for all children. It will be important for teachers to know which experiences have been helpful and positive and which ones have been negative. All this builds a picture of how the children in the class perceive reading. It provides teachers with the knowledge to sculpt the nature of the reading teaching that will occur in the class to suit all the children with their different needs.

Children's reflection

How does the child view her/himself as a reader? Can they reflect on their own development as a reader? These questions can be answered during reading conferences (see below) and through informal discussions with the child on other occasions. The child needs to know that bringing their own experiences to a text will assist in the ability to read and enjoy it.

Strategies

In Chapter 2 we described the cueing strategies necessary for children to read successfully – semantic, syntactic and grapho-phonic.

Semantic cueing is when readers draw on the text but also on their own knowledge of the context and/or environment within which the narrative takes place. Pictures that illustrate that grass is green and children's own knowledge of grass in the real world will assist children in reading descriptions of gardens.

Syntactic cues again draw on what children know, but this time what they know about language and how utterances are structured grammatically. This too helps children predict the next word in a text.

Grapho-phonic cueing is used by knowing sound–symbol correspondences and the visual knowledge of letter combinations and sight vocabulary. Here the children rely on the text to help them read the next word in a book. Often children also draw on their knowledge of phonology here, i.e. how a word sounds, and additionally use their knowledge of other words, how they sound and how they appear on the page (the sound/symbol relationship) to make analogous connections.

In addition to teaching about the processes of reading, part of a teacher's job is to ensure children are learning to use these cues, and when they are not, to provide experiences that encourage them to do so. This can be carried out through shared and guided reading and writing opportunities as discussed earlier, as well as through individual support.

Teachers can hear when children are using the cues through informal observations of their reading, but it is very useful for teachers to find more systematic ways of recording the development of the children's reading strategies. This can be achieved by half-termly 'running records'.

Running records

Running records are a way of making an analysis of children's use of cueing strategies. It is a simplified version of something called miscue analysis (Goodman 1973) which is often used for older children and was developed by the late Marie Clay (1985). Running records work well with children in Key Stages 1 and 2 who are already beginning to read independently aloud. It enables teachers to focus upon the errors (miscues) that children make while they read aloud. The teacher records the strategies the child is using (semantic, grapho-phonic, syntactic) and the child's response, their understanding, fluency, self-correction and expression.

Running records are the professional's assessment tool and provide extremely important information about the child's development. The teacher chooses a book that is known to the child, but is not so well-known that the child can recite it without reading the text. Teachers often photocopy the section of the text that they want the child to read. The teacher and child have a copy. The teacher reads aloud from the section before the part that will be read by the child. The child takes over and while the child reads the teacher must try not to intervene but provide help if really needed. The teacher records the miscues on her copy of the reading. Afterwards the teacher talks to the child about the text to establish the nature of the response that the child provides. Later the miscues are analysed by the teacher and from this data the teacher is better prepared to tailor the teaching and learning the child requires. The whole process is undertaken informally and should be as much like a normal one-to-one sharing of a book as possible. Of course, it is useful to make an audio recording of the reading so teachers can analyse the reading at their 'leisure'.

Possible miscues include:

- non-response to word – write NR above word;
- substitution – write the substituted word above the word in the text, e.g. said (substitute) shouted (text);
- omission – misses out a word – circle the word missed out;
- insertion – adds a word – write I.
- reversal – 'tightly was he pinned down' to 'tightly he was pinned down';
- self-correction – goes back to correct word read differently to what is in the text – write SC above word;
- hesitation – write H above the word;
- repetition – repeats word or phrase;
- make a stroke for all words read as they appear in the text.

The teacher's analysis will involve discerning between positive and negative miscues. Miscues are negative when the general meaning and coherence of the text is lost by what the child reads aloud. Readers, both experienced and inexperienced, miscue all the time when they read. This is normal reading behaviour. Readers do not always read every word as it is written down. There is nothing wrong with this. It only becomes a problem when the meaning is lost.

Miscues are also negative when it is clear that the reader is not drawing on one or all of the cueing strategies to assist fluency – hesitations, non-response and insertion or substitution of words that detract from the meaning would indicate a need for more strategies. Positive miscues include self-correction, insertions, reversals or substitutions that do not detract from the meaning. Teachers should not feel the need to correct these kinds of miscues. They are positive and demonstrate a child's growing maturity and confidence as a reader.

Grapho-phonic strategies

Dombey and Moustafa (1998) drawing on Frith (1985) describe how phonics learning can be viewed in three distinct phases – logographic (beginning at around three), analytic and orthographic. We are wary of investing too much trust in phases or stages of learning; however, it may be useful to discuss learning phonics in terms of a conceptual framework to help make abstractions about how children might develop these print-based strategies. We also want to emphasise that significant forms of reading begin when childred are much younger than this, in informal and sometimes unmonitored contexts, as described in earlier chapters.

However, from around the age of three, according to the model presented by Dombey and Moustafa, it will be possible to see children beginning to learn to read print. They contend that during this logographic phase children need plenty of support from adults and more exprienced readers to begin to read the words on the page. In this phase, children begin to recognise words and learn them as whole entities. Dombey and Moustafa describe what children begin to be able to do in this phase:

> They may recognise repeated words and phrases, and they generally begin to develop a 'mental lexicon' of known words from these familiar texts and from the print around them. Their experience of reading with others teaches them about directionality and they may develop a sense of one-to-one correspondence in the context of books they know well. They are also likely to play with sounds of language and enjoy rhyme and patterned language. But they have no way of processing new words and need support (e.g. from shared reading) to approach unfamiliar texts. At the same time they may be learning the letters of the alphabet, and just beginning to use this knowledge in their early writing and in their reading. (Dombey and Moustafa 1998: 24)

As we have mentioned elsewhere in this book, conceptualising learning in discrete stages has its dangers as those children who do not meet the criteria at these ages begin to be thought of as not 'normal' in some way and a deficit view of individual children begins to be built up. However, the criteria identified here are broad and should not be considered definitive in any way.

The analytic phase is marked by the children beginning to be able to learn by analogy. Through their awareness of alphabet letters and their knowledge of onset and rime they begin to be able to relate unknown words to the words they already know. Although they will still be learning new words by the logographic principle, this new use of analogy will be providing another strategy for reading unknown words.

> Children will now be able to take an interest in the shapes and structures of words, and to notice similarities between words. Initially they will be recognising chunks of language (e.g. words within words, syllables, common spelling patterns) rather than looking at individual letters. They find it easy to perceive common rimes – rhyming endings that are spelt the same, such as j-am and S-am, and this helps them to read and spell new words by analogy. (Dombey and Moustafa 1998: 28)

In the orthographic phase children begin to identify words from their spellings. In terms of their grapho-phonic cueing strategies, children will no longer need to process new words bit by bit. They will now be able to draw on a growing repertory of spelling patterns to recognise words rapidly.

> As children move from dependence to independence in reading and begin to be able to attempt to read unfamiliar texts, they will need to draw on a range of strategies to help them read and write fluently. They will be looking even more closely at print and learning to observe the ways in which words are constructed and spelled. They are also learning to orchestrate the different cueing systems (semantic, syntactic and grapho-phonic) in texts and to read the print with growing confidence and accuracy. (Dombey and Moustafa 1998: 30)

Early concepts of print

For very young children, any kind of formal assessment is inappropriate, but Marie Clay (1979) has offered guidance to teachers on monitoring young children's understanding about print. We would like to add here that the first consideration should be a child's interest in books, print and stories. In addition, Clay suggests that teachers can assess if young children:

- can identify the front of a book;
- know that the print informs the reader what to say;
- can identify where the reader begins the reading and in which direction they need to go (directionality);
- know what happens when one gets to the end of one line – in English we return to the left;
- can identify the first and last letter;
- have one-to-one correspondence – the child recognises words in the wrong order;
- knows that readers start reading on the left page before the right (in most cases!).

As the children become more experienced, teachers will be interested in their awareness of punctuation, upper and lower case letters, the difference between the meaning of 'word' and 'letter'. This is in addition to continuing to observe and understand children's attitudes and interests in books and stories and reading generally.

Everyday assessments

We believe, like others, that evidence of children's reading should be recorded in words not numbers (Barrs 1990; Grainger and Tod 2000). Assigning a number to a child (as in the use of National Curriculum Levels) to represent the development a child is making is insulting to children and fails to honour the richness of learning and progress that individual children make over a short period. Record-keeping formats that were developed by Myra Barrs (1988) and her colleagues at the Centre for Literacy in Primary Education (CLPE) were a particularly valuable way of managing ongoing assessment. They encouraged a range of informal methods of assessing children's development. Below, in common with the work of CLPE, we provide ideas that teachers can use to develop a holistic understanding of a child's development as a reader.

Guided reading

Small-group work with children will enable teachers to observe how particular children in the group operate and engage with independent reading activities.

A notebook can be used to record how the child is coping with the task independently and how the child manages to feed back and share her thoughts with the rest of the children afterwards.

Reading conference

One-to-one conversations can create rich opportunities to discover more about individual children in the class. They provide a forum for children to talk about their likes and dislikes with reading and provide an opportunity for teachers to learn about their attitudes and their ability to reflect on their own development. These can take the form of informal chats, but teachers may wish to do as Barrs and Browne (1991) recommend and create two occasions a year when individual children and the teacher sit down for a longer and more focused talk. Some teachers find it helpful to note the children's comments as a record to provide a focus for the next discussion to observe any changes. Children who have English as an additional language will also be able to discuss the reading they have been undertaking in their mother tongue or other languages they know. In addition, all children will be able to talk about the stories they have been reading or viewing. It is important to be aware of children's interests in popular culture in order to build on these in the classroom.

Reading diaries

A teacher's reading diary is usually kept in a file of some kind and consists of dated comments that have come from observations or conversations with the child. Opportunities often occur in classrooms when individual children can be seen participating in reading in different contexts. The diary can be used to record significant events or progress observed at these times. The diary needs to be in an easily accessible place so these moments can be captured. The diary can record behaviours that provide evidence of developing confidence and independence, and strategies, knowledge and understanding in reading. The diary will slowly accumulate useful and interesting observations that can be later discussed in parent consultations and reading conferences with the children. They are also very useful for report writing. Other teachers use Post-it stickers for these moment-by-moment observations and formalise them at the end of a day or at the end of a week.

Reading journals

Reading journals are not only a useful way of understanding children's development, but also great fun for children and teachers. They are often used in relation to home–school reading systems. Reading journals are small writing books within which the children write comments about the books they are reading. Some teachers also encourage the parents to contribute and describe their thoughts on the book, its meaning and how they have enjoyed it. The power of reading journals is in the way a dialogue is constructed between the three journalists. The best journals are 'assessment-of-writing-free'. The teacher never corrects spelling or comments on the handwriting. They are also the journals where the teacher responds to the child as an equal and a fellow reading enthusiast. The children we have worked with really enjoy this relationship with the teacher and this is shown by the comments. Some can be very amusing. Children will write comments about the books they have been reading and will feel confident to comment on the teacher's reading style or the voices they assume to depict the characters. Some can be rather critical! The diaries will inform the teacher about the child's attitude to reading and the books they are enjoying reading. It provides teachers with knowledge about the books the children have read, and makes it possible for the teacher to suggest others that may enrich their reading tastes or offer new genres to discover.

Informal observations

Research into literacy pedagogy (Medwell et al. 1998) tells us that effective teachers include 'the continuous monitoring of children's progress through the tasks provided and the use of informal assessment to give the basis for teaching and reporting on this progress' (p. 5). This very influential research commissioned by the Teacher Training Agency describes in some detail what effective teachers do when they assess their children:

- record the reading strategies the children were using;
- make notes of children's enjoyment of books;
- discuss children's reading diaries;
- work with small groups of children 'probing, questioning and supporting' (p. 41);
- make observations and take notes in informal ways.

The researchers comment that the effective teachers of literacy in their sample 'were less likely ... to place reliance upon tests for their assessment of literacy' (p. 41). However, this was twelve years ago, and tests and National Curriculum Levels have forced many teachers to conceptualise learning in terms of numbers. We hope the teachers in this study are still using the same methods as recommended in 1998.

Final thoughts on assessment

We want to finish this chapter with a quote from a book by Peter Geekie, Brian Cambourne and Phil Fitzsimmons (1999) called *Understanding Literacy Development* for which we both have a great deal of respect. In it, they comment on what a seemingly extraordinary feat it is for a teacher to know what 30 or so children know about literacy in a classroom. Yet the writers of the book draw comparisons with the volume of knowledge we have of our large networks of friends and relatives. We remember the things we have shared and disclosed to each other and all these experiences build up a picture of those people. At this point it is worth quoting these writers at length because they sum up perfectly why we know all this about those we care for and why it is possible to know a great deal about the children in our classrooms.

> But we only remember such things because we interact with these people individually in mutually intelligible conversations in familiar settings. The teacher's knowledge of the children in his or her class has the same basis. If the only activities in the classroom are teacher-directed lessons and closely supervised set work which is evaluated in terms of preconceived standards of correctness, teachers will learn little about the children in their care. But if many opportunities exist for teachers to talk individually with the children in their classes they will soon develop what Brown (1980) calls an 'apperceptive mass' of knowledge about each child which can be tapped at appropriate times to assist in decision-making, problem-solving and even just making sense of casual conversational exchanges. The importance of this aspect of learning cannot be over-emphasised. (p. 33)

As we said at the start of this chapter, the assessment of children's development should reflect the forms of society we aspire towards, based on fairness, genuine democracy and love. The classrooms where teachers work wear their 'assessment on their sleeves' and reflect their beliefs about children, education and society. Teachers need to resist the forms of teaching and assessment that run counter to these aspirations.

Conclusion

We have tried to pack this chapter with ideas for assessment of reading in early years classrooms. Like every chapter in this book, we have also attempted to provide 'food for thought' about the choices that are made about the pedagogies that are used with the young. For assessment, we have chosen to discuss the relation between how one assesses children and the society it reflects. We critique the latest advice from governments and we make our suggestions based on a long line of research and practice.

Further reading

Hall, K. (2003) *Listening to Stephen Read: Multiple Perspectives on Literacy*. Buckingham: Open University Press.

Johnstone, P. and Costello, P. (2009) 'Principles for literacy assessment', in F. Fletcher-Campbell, J. Soler and G. Reid (eds), *Approaching Difficulties in Literacy Development: Assessment, Pedagogy and Programmes*. London: Sage.

10

Conclusions: principles and practice

In this chapter we aim:

- to summarise our argument on the teaching and learning of reading;
- to discuss Shannon's (2000) analysis of how reading teaching policy has begun to reflect the logic of fast-paced business, where efficiency takes precedence over quality and care;
- to describe the seven principles of learning that have resonance across this book and in the ideas we have offered throughout the chapters;
- to conclude with Ken Goodman's perspectives on the use of phonics in learning to read.

Throughout this book it will have become apparent that the authors have particular views about learning and that these views on learning directly influence our understanding about how children learn to read. We suspect that if readers have managed to arrive at this part of the book, they too probably share these beliefs. It will be clear to readers that we do not contend that reading is a series of skills used across texts, and that these skills simply need to be taught to beginner readers as part of a repeated instructed process by an adult expert. We also do not believe that children read simply because they have been taught to do so by systematic and explicit instruction of phonics. For us and others (for example, Geekie et al. 1999), these ideas, which we understand from research to be incorrect, implicitly reveal a belief about learning and children's minds and promote a perspective that learning involves a process of transmission of knowledge and skills from teacher to child. Our position is based around the knowledge that learning does not just occur in classrooms, but that it happens all the time. Learning is a social practice, best achieved in meaningful interactions with others, some of whom will be more experienced and interested than others. Educators need to learn from the forms of interaction that can occur outside of classrooms to help understand the effective ways that young people can learn inside them. With our perspectives in mind, drawn from research knowledge and understanding of theories of learning as well as experiences of teaching children to read, this chapter raises the problems associated with recent government initiatives to introduce 'efficiency' into reading teaching and highlights its detrimental effects on children and teachers. We go on by drawing on Geekie et al.'s (1999) seven principles of learning with which we make direct links with reading pedagogy. Finally, we say some last words about the future for early reading teaching and look forward to a future where teachers see them themselves as 'activists' (Day and Sachs 2004) as part of their professional responsibilities.

Efficiency

Shannon (2000) draws attention to what he describes as the growing 'efficiency movement' in reading teaching. He argues that approaches to reading, since the early twentieth century, have been copying the logic of production that exists in modern capitalist states. This logic states that in order to reduce risk to business and capital and to ensure the maximisation of profits, all aspects of industry must become as predictable as possible. From this perspective, work is conceptualised as a rational process. There is no space for any form of spirituality and emotion and therefore productive forces must be organised accordingly. Shannon (2000) quotes Ravitch when she says: 'Teachers don't need creativity. Teachers need to use methods that have proved successful.' In other words, all the emotive and human individualism, talent and motivations must be removed from the process of reading teaching.

> In this way, raw materials, the environment and the workers become simply factors in the planning and organisation of production – none require any special consideration and treatment. (Shannon 2000: 1).

The use of highly prescriptive teaching which will sometimes use teaching scripts or new technological equipment such as whiteboards to provide the actual lessons that have been constructed by private companies are justified, according to Shannon, by this business logic of efficiency. More frighteningly, these processes become to appear natural and inevitable to those working in schools. After all, from teachers' perspectives, it would be sensible to use these prescribed methods to increase the chances of higher test scores and avoid the prospect of punishment (Johnstone and Costello 2009).

Shannon (2000) draws on the concept of reification to explain the plight of our teachers in schools. Reification is the process by which some form of abstraction is treated as if it were an immutable procedure. When the logic of business and capitalist efficiency is used in the process of education, teachers tend to lose sight of the fact that the teaching of reading is really a human process. Furthermore, reading defined in these closed ways has the consequence of freezing teachers' knowledge about the processes of teaching and learning. When test scores are reified into principally what all learning really is, then a teacher's work is closed down into a state of efficient and effective delivery of reading instruction. The teaching of phonics through 'teacher-safe' schemes to all children in a vulgar 'sheep-dipping' style, where all children are provided with the same experiences, is what this book categorically opposes. A Year 2 teacher (Lambirth 2007b: 82) in conversation with us about how teachers' attitudes to reading pedagogy have changed in her school and in others described the processes involved:

> ... all the pressures you get from publishers, the types of books that are coming out and courses that are pushed in schools over and over again. 'These are the resources you must have'. Teachers do feel the pressure from that and want to buy those things that 'will' save their children from failure. Pressure is coming in that way as well. They are hearing about these methods, when they may not know the background behind them, have done no research but take them on board because they think 'this is what I must do'. There are whole groups of teachers from a range of age phases who tend to adopt every kind of initiative, scheme and document because they are frightened to let go of them. This material becomes like a safety blanket now because I think they have lost their values, they have had them taken away.

These attitudes, fears and responses from teachers are symptomatic of what Shannon describes as an efficiency model of education. It dishonours teachers and their ability to respond professionally in an informed way to the needs of individual children. Through the threat of punishment and sanction, governments have managed to reify efficiency methods. We hope this book will form part of the 'fightback' towards a more human, social and professional approach to children's early reading. We know that many teachers still feel invigorated by the prospect of reclaiming their professionalism. It is to those teachers to whom we dedicate this book.

Principles of learning

As part of our conclusion to this book on early reading and phonics, we will make some direct connections with our suggestions for teachers in this book and some principles of learning that Geekie et al. (1999) describe. These principles lie behind most of the activities we recommend in this book as it has studied forms of learning that look further than efficiency as justification for their use.

The first principle is that learning can often be a mutual accomplishment. Teachers and children tend to work together when learning is achieved (Rogoff 1989). As we have just said, successful teachers do not just transmit knowledge and skills to children, and the children do not just receive this information passively. On the contrary, children will unconsciously sculpt the nature and form of the teacher's intervention by the pace of their learning, guiding the adult to erect the necessary support and scaffolding for the child's benefit. Learning is collaborative and not teacher-driven. One of the roles of the reading teacher is to understand the individual child's background, experience, knowledge and confidence. The teaching is tailored from this form of understanding.

The second principle is that children can often learn through guided participation (Rogoff 1989). We discussed the importance of children's participation in Chapter 2. By children participating in reading activities – listening to books, reading along, and joining in with texts – they begin to understand the purposes of reading. David (2007) describes how this participation manifests itself in early readers learning to use print:

> … babies and young children are eager to understand and be able to use the power of print … Fifteen-month-old Sebastian points to the print in his favourite picture book, babbling to himself as he does. He has heard the narrative in this text so many times and has seen some of his family members sliding a finger along the print. He knows these marks mean something significant that he loves to hear and, in his own way, repeat. Oliver, when a little older, voluntarily pointed out all the 'Os' in a book sharing with a grandparent – not yet 3, he knew 'O' was a significant symbol for him. (p.15)

So much of everyday life for Sebastian and Oliver has revolved around participation with texts that both these children had independently begun to learn the significance of print. Their environment and the children's determination to engage in these meaningful activities with print had guided these children's participation. Our book asks teachers to construct the interior of their classrooms in a way that will develop this form of guided participation, by creating opportunities for children to develop their literacy in meaningful ways. A culture of reading and a love of books can be developed in a classroom as we described in Chapter 5. This must happen for all children in all socio-cultural and economic circumstances. We strongly believe that it is wrong-headed to assume that children from poor backgrounds where books are not an everyday part of the culture need a non-participatory programme of teaching. It is not uncommon for educationalists to profess that differentiation of approach to children should be based on socio-economic background and status. For example, in a recent *Guardian* article (Scott 2010), an educationalist is reported as saying:

> Those from socio-economically disadvantaged backgrounds need good, sharp, upfront teacher-driven interactive phonics right from the minute they start school. Middle-class kids who come with quite a lot of book knowledge do better when they are given self-directed activities at the beginning, and a more sharp, hard input of more complex phonics later.

We feel that these comments seem to suggest that the poor and/or those who come from alternative socio-economic backgrounds and cultures to middle-class people must be given schooling's version of 'tough-love' from the tenderest age. We ask 'Why should the poor have to undergo "sharp" phonics teaching so young?' Surely, what proves to be more conducive to learning to read are the kinds of guided participatory opportunities with books that many children have experienced before coming to school and which we have recommended throughout this book? The educationalist seems to be claiming that with such rich experiences children would not have to face the sharp pointed finger of phonics teaching until later. Of course, if individual children, as they grow older, need to have their attention drawn to the print, then so be it, but it is clearly misguided to assume that all young children from particular social backgrounds need 'teacher-driven interactive phonics right from the minute they start school'.

The third principle is that children profit from the support of more competent people. Wood (1988) has shown that children are 'novices of life' in general and they need the assistance of more knowledgeable others to cope with novel experiences and demands. What in effect happens when teachers work alongside children in forms of guided participation is that the adults allow the children to use the capacity they already have to complete tasks – a borrowing of the adult's consciousness to allow children to succeed in tasks that they could not manage on their own. Of course, as we have mentioned before, this is what Vygotsky (1978) called the 'zone of proximal development'. Teachers assist in developing the abilities that children possess already. The children can find the means to activate their skills and knowledge with help from a more experienced other. In addition, this assistance is provided to help children understand what the intention of the activity may be. The forms of classroom experience and teaching that we suggest in this book draw on this principle. We have suggested creating an overall environment that promotes the affordances and pleasures of reading; we have described the ways teachers can tailor their interventions to children's needs based upon what is known about the child's experiences and development from home and at school, and we have tried to express the need to present and promote reading as a form of pleasure and play.

Geekie et al.'s (1999) fourth principle is that good teaching is contingent instruction. Like Wood (1988), they contend that teaching involves 'leading as following'; it is essentially a responsive act. Teachers are effective 'child-watchers' – they sculpt their teaching from what they have observed in children's behaviours. Teachers only offer the support that they know the child needs. As children begin to start reading and drawing on particular strategies they are given the space to practise on their own. As Bruner (1983) commented, 'where there was once an observer, let there now be a participant'. Teaching becomes a process of 'handover' and a transfer of control. The move to independent opportunities is crucial in this apprenticeship approach to learning and learning to read. Direct instruction or adult control of the learning in all situations is as inappropriate in the teaching of reading as it is in any other form of learning. Good teachers lead by following.

The fifth principle is about the importance of quality interactions. Interaction in itself is not enough. Rogoff (1990) recommends that teachers plan classroom activities in collaboration with the children. She contends that an expert must be available to work with the novice, but this alone is not enough. In a study cited by Geekie et al. (1999) (Radziszewska and Rogoff 1988), the collaborative nature of adult–child pairs contributed to better performance. The partners had shared and guided the decisions that were taking place within an activity and consequently had achieved their intentions. The collaborative partners were seen to perform better than those who had used less collaboration. Once again, we have tried to make suggestions for practice in this book which are guided by this principle. Our chapter on the teacher's role and the environments that he or she needs to construct in early years classrooms demonstrates the power of creating a more democratic situation and ethos.

Principle six is that language is the means through which self-regulation of learning behaviour develops. All learning will be assisted when the experts demonstrate the essential processes involved. This is no different to learning to read. The educational landscape of classrooms needs to be scattered with talk. Opportunities to talk around books and texts in general are able to demonstrate the kinds of experiences, processes and skills that need to be in operation when reading takes place. Opportunities like this occur in independent guided, shared and one-to-one reading. Teachers begin to demonstrate the essential processes of reading when they show the children their enthusiasm for stories and how they like to read them and talk about the pictures and what happens in them. This enthusiasm and the content of the teacher's talk helps children understand what is expected and what needs to be done to extract this much satisfaction from books. Children then begin to use language to regulate their own development as readers, and assisted by the teacher in all the different activities in routines and through carefully tailored teaching, the child enters that culture of reading.

Principle seven says that learning depends upon the negotiation of meaning. As Lloyd (1990) has shown, in connection with the previous principles we have outlined here adults are not just a source of expert information. Experts become an extension of the learner's own cognitive and communicative system. Adults, experts and teachers focus the learner's attention on the specific detail of what needs to be learned. They remind the learner what needs to be held in the memory and what has gone before and alerts them to their successes and failures. Meanings about the world and what needs to be learned are jointly constructed: 'learning proceeds smoothly because the focus is on the construction of meaning and the maintenance of communication' (Geekie et al. 1999: 1). Here again, negotiation is highlighted as being significant for learning. Learning is social and collaborative in nature. Children cannot learn by the transmission alone of information from the adult. Most new knowledge and skills must be positioned within a meaningful context for the children and be provided in an environment that best resembles how we know children learn best.

A last word on phonics from the expert

Throughout this book we have drawn on many great names in the teaching of reading. One that has reoccurred time and time again is that of Ken Goodman. We want to end this book with some of the specific things he says about phonics. In his book *Phonics Phacts* (1993) there is a great deal of wisdom provided on how teachers can use phonics in the classroom as well as useful insights on the history and politics of phonics in schools. Goodman's view is that teaching phonics is insufficient to make readers of non-readers and if children do come to read through exposure to prescribed 'phonics-first' reading programmes they do so because of the 'ability of most children to learn language, including reading and writing, in spite of the obstacles put in their way' (1993: 107). Goodman does not wholly reject phonics, but instead wants to put it in its proper place. It is worth quoting Goodman at length here:

> What we've learned from the study of language development, both oral and written, is that language is easy to learn when we deal with the whole of it as we use it functionally to make sense. Little children are understanding and making themselves understood in oral language long before they fully control the sound system. That's because they learn language in the context of its own use. Children learn written language in the same way. They may learn the names of letters as they're learning to read, and even have some sense of how they relate to sounds. But they can learn the abstract phonics system only in the context of trying to make sense of print. They're good at learning language when it's in authentic, meaningful context. They are not very good at learning abstractions out of context. (p. 109)

As we have argued in this book, Goodman believes that phonics is an intrinsic part of reading. Yet he argues that when it becomes a method of teaching reading by teaching letter-to-sound correspondence out of context we make fundamental mistakes. For Goodman, by teaching this way, reading turns from being a process of making meaning and sense into one of saying sounds for letters. It ignores what children already come to school knowing about language and contributes to the possibility of children beginning to doubt themselves and becoming confused about their own learning. By teaching phonics out of context we distort it as it is removed from the meaning and structure of language. Meaning and the function of reading are relegated to second place in favour of these kinds of abstractions.

Goodman is one of many of our heroes and heroines that have continued to speak out for a learning that honours children's intelligence and capabilities and their right to have these traits recognised through the forms of pedagogy they are exposed to in schools. This book has tried to present a model for the teaching of reading that takes children's natural and cultural abilities seriously. We hope that when teachers and student teachers read this book it will contribute to a professionalism that is based on an understanding of learning championed by us and which continues to have a proud and noble record within the educational research community and among knowledgeable and creative teachers.

Further reading

Geekie, P., Cambourne, B. and Fitzsimmons, P. (1999) *Understanding Literacy Development*. Stoke-on-Trent: Trentham Books.

Shannon, P. (2000) 'A Marxist reading of reading education', *Cultural Logic*, 4: 1–13.

References

Aardema, V. (1986) *Bringing the Rain to Kapiti Plain*. London: Macmillan Picturemac.

Adams, M. J. (1990) *Beginning to Read, Thinking and Learning About Print*. Cambridge, MA: MIT Press.

Alexander, R. (ed.) (2010) *Children, Their World, Their Education: Final Report and Recommendations of the Cambridge Primary Review*. Abingdon: Routledge.

Barrs, M. (1988) *The Primary Language Record Handbook for Teachers*. London: CLPE.

Barrs, M. (1990) *Words Not Numbers: Assessment in English*. Sheffield: NAAE/NATE.

Barrs, M. and Cork, V. (2001) *The Reader in the Writer*. London: CLPE.

Barrs, M. and Ellis, S. (1998) *The Core Book: A Structured Approach to Using Books with the Reading Curriculum*. London: CLPE.

Barrs, M. and Meek Spencer, M. (2007) 'Inquiry into meaning: a conversation', in K. Goouch and A. Lambirth (eds), *Understanding Phonics and the Teaching of Reading: Critical Perspectives*. Maidenhead: Open University Press/McGraw-Hill.

Barrs, M. and Thomas, A. (1991) *The Reading Book*. London: CLPE.

Barton, D. (1994) *Literacy: An Introduction to the Ecology of Written Language*. Oxford: Blackwell.

Beckett, F. (2000) 'Couldn't do better', *Guardian Education*, 19 September.

Bernstein, B. (1996) *Pedagogy, Symbolic Control and Identity*. London: Taylor & Francis.

Bernstein, B. (2003) 'Social class and pedagogic practice', in *The Structuring of Pedagogic Discourse*, Vol. IV: *Class, Codes and Control*. Abingdon: Routledge.

Blakemore, S. J. and Frith, U. (2005) *The Learning Brain: Lessons for Education*. Oxford: Blackwell.

Brice Heath, S. (1983) *Ways with Words*. Cambridge: Cambridge University Press.

Britton, J. (1982) *Prospect and Retrospect*. London: Heinemann.

Bromley, H. (2000) *Book Based Reading Games*. London: CLPE.

Brown, R. (1980) 'The maintenance of conversation', in D. Olson (ed.), *The Social Foundations of Language and Thought*. London: W.W.Norton.

Bruner, J. (1960) *The Process of Education*. Cambridge, MA: Harvard University Press.

Bruner, J. (1983) *Child's Talk: Learning to Use Language*. Oxford: Oxford University Press.

Bruner, J. (1996) *The Culture of Education*. Cambridge, MA: Harvard University Press.

Bryan, H. (2004) 'Constructs of teacher professionalism within a changing literary landscape', *Literacy*, 38 (3): 141–8.

Bryant, P. and Bradley, L. (1985) *Children's Reading Problems*. Oxford: Blackwell.

Bullock, A. (1975) *A Language for Life*. London: HMSO.

Burkard, T. (1999) *The End of Illiteracy? The Holy Grail of Clackmannanshire*. London: Centre for Policy Studies.

Chambers, A. (1991) *The Reading Environment*. Stroud: Thimble Press.

Chambers, A. (1993) *Tell Me. Children Reading and Talk*. Stroud: Thimble Press.

Chittenden, E. and Salinger, T. with Bussis, A. M. (2001) *Inquiry into Meaning: An Investigation of Learning to Read*, revised edn. New York: Teachers College Press.

Chomsky, N. (1972) *Language and Mind*. New York: Harcourt Brace Jovanovich.

Clarke, M. (1976) *Young Fluent Readers: What Can They Teach Us?* London: Heinemann.

Clay, M. (1979) *The Early Detection of Reading Difficulties*, 2nd edn. Aukland: Heinemann.

Clay, M. (1985) *The Early Detection of Reading Difficulties*, 3rd edn. Auckland: Heinemann.

Clay, M. (1998) *By Different Paths to Common Outcomes*. York, ME: Stenhouse Publishers.

Cole, M. (1996) *Cultural Psychology: A Once and Future Discipline*. Cambridge, MA: Harvard University Press.

Corden, R. (2000) *Literacy and Understanding Through Talk*. Maidenhead: Open University Press.

Cremin, T. (2007) 'Revisiting reading for pleasure: diversity, delight and desire', in K. Goouch and A. Lambirth (eds), *Understanding Phonics and the Teaching of Reading*. Maidenhead: Open University Press/McGraw-Hill.

Cremin, T., Bearne, E., Goodwin, P. and Mottram, M. (2008) 'Primary teachers as readers', *English in Education*, 42 (1): 1–16.

Crooks, T. J. (1988) 'The impact of classroom evaluation practices on students', *Review of Educational Research*, 58: 438–81.

David, T. (2007) 'What is early childhood for?', in K. Goouch and A. Lambirth (eds), *Understanding Phonics and the Teaching of Reading: Critical Perspectives*. Maidenhead: Open University Press/McGraw-Hill.

David, T., Goouch, K., Powell, S. and Abbott, L. (2003) *Birth to Three Matters: A Review of the Literature*. Nottingham: DfES Publications.

David. T., Raban, B., Ure, C., Goouch, K., Jago, M., Barriere, I. and Lambirth, A. (2000) *Making Sense of Early Literacy: A Practitioner's Perspective*. Stoke-on-Trent: Trentham Books.

Day, C. and Sachs, J. (2004) *International Handbook of Continuing Professional Development of Teachers*. Buckingham: Open University Press.

Deacon, T. (1997) *The Symbolic Species: The Co-Evolution of Language and the Human Brain*. London: Penguin.

Department for Children, Schools and Families (2007) *The Early Years Foundation Stage*. London: DfES Publications.

Department for Children, Schools and Families (2009a) *Introduction to Assessing Pupil Progress*. http://nationalstrategies.standards.dcsf.gov.uk/node/160673?uc%20=%20force_uj.

Department for Children, Schools and Families (2009b) *The Simple View of Reading*. http://nationalstrategies.standards.dcsf.gov.uk/node/20162 (accessed 21 February 2010).

Department for Education and Employment (1998) *The National Literacy Strategy: A Framework for Teaching*. London: DfEE.

Department for Education and Employment (2000a) *Progression into Phonics*. London: DfEE.

Department for Education and Employment (2000b) 'Inner-City Schools Improve Faster to Narrow the Literacy and Numeracy Gap as Test Results Confirm Government Target'. DfEE press release, 20 September.

Department for Education and Skills (2003) *Excellence and Enjoyment: A Strategy for Primary Schools*. London: DfES Publications.

Department for Education and Skills (2004) *Five Year Strategy for Children and Learners*. London: HMSO.

Department for Education and Skills (2006) *Independent Review of the Teaching of Early Reading* (The Rose Review). London: DfES.

Dombey, H. and Moustafa, M. (1998) *Whole to Part Phonics: How Children Learn to Read and Spell*. London: CLPE.

Durkheim, E. (1956) *Education and Society*. New York: Free Press.

Durkin, D. (1966) *Children Who Read Early: Two Longitudinal Studies*. New York: Teachers College Press.

Dweck, C. S. (1999) *Self-Theories: Their Role in Motivation, Personality and Development*. Philadelphia, PA: Psychology Press.

Ehri, L. C. (1987) 'Learning to read and spell words', *Journal of Reading Behaviour*, 19: 5–31.

Ehri, L. C. (1995) 'Phases of development in learning to read words by sight', *Journal of Research in Reading*, 18 (2): 116–25.

Fisher, R. and Lewis, M. (1999) 'Anticipation or trepidation? Teachers' views on the Literacy Hour', *Reading*, 33 (1): 23–8.

Frater, G. (2000) 'Observed in practice. English in the National Literacy Strategy: some reflections', *Reading*, 34 (3): 107–13.

Freire, P. (1972) *Pedagogy of the Oppressed*. London: Penguin.

Frith, U. (1985) 'Developmental dyslexia', in K. E. Patterson (ed.), *Surface Dyslexia*. Hove: Lawrence Erlbaum Associates.

Gale, T. and Densmore, K. (2000) *Just Schooling: Explorations in the Cultural Politics of Teaching*. Maidenhead: Open University Press/McGraw-Hill.

Gee, J. P. (2001) 'What is literacy?', in P. Shannon (ed.), *Becoming Political Too: New Readings and Writings on the Politics of Literacy Education*. Portsmouth, NH: Heinemann.

Gee, J. P. (2004) *Situated Language Learning: A Critique of Traditional Schooling*. Abingdon: Routledge.

Geekie, P., Cambourne, B. and Fitzsimmons, P. (1999) *Understanding Literacy Development*. Stoke-on-Trent: Trentham Books.

Goodman, K. (1967) 'Reading: a psycholinguistic guessing game', *Journal of the Reading Specialist*, 4: 126–35.

Goodman, K. (1973) 'Psycholinguistic universals in the reading process', in F. Smith (ed.), *Psycholinguistics and Reading*. New York: Holt, Rinehart & Winston.

Goodman, K. (1993) *Phonics Phacts: A Common Sense Look at the Most Controversial Issue Affecting Today's Classrooms*. Portsmouth, NH: Heinemann.

Goodman, K. (1996) *On Reading*. Portsmouth, NH: Heinemann.

Goouch, K. (2007) 'Understanding educational discourse: attending to multiple voices', in K. Goouch and A. Lambirth (eds), *Understanding Phonics and the Teaching of Reading: Critical Perspectives*. Maidenhead: Open University Press/McGraw-Hill.

Goouch, K. and Lambirth, A. (2007a) 'Introduction: sound and fury', in K. Goouch and A. Lambirth (eds), *Understanding Phonics and the Teaching of Reading: Critical Perspectives*. Maidenhead: Open University Press/McGraw-Hill.

Goouch, K. and Lambirth, A. (2007b) *Understanding Phonics and the Teaching of Reading: Critical Perspectives*. Maidenhead: Open University Press/McGraw-Hill.

Goswami, U. (2002) 'Rhymes, phonemes and learning to read: interpreting recent research', in M. Cook (ed.), *Perspectives on the Teaching and Learning of Phonics*. Royston: UK Literacy Association.

Goswami, U. (2005) 'Synthetic phonics and learning to read: a cross language perspective', *Educational Psychology in Practice*, 21 (4): 273–82.

Goswami, U. (2007) 'Learning to read across languages: the role of phonics and synthetic phonics', in K. Goouch and A. Lambirth (eds), *Understanding Phonics and the Teaching of Reading: Critical Perspectives*. Maidenhead: Open University Press/McGraw-Hill.

Goswami, U. and Bryant, P. (1990) *Phonological Skills and Learning to Read*. Hove: Psychology Press.

Graham, J. (2004) *Cracking Good Picture Books: Teaching Literature at Key Stage 1*. Sheffield: NATE.

Grainger, T. and Todd, J. (2000) *Inclusive Educational Practice: Literacy*. London: David Fulton.

Grainger, T., Goouch, K. and Lambirth, A. (2005) *Creativity and Writing: Developing Voice and Verve in the Classroom*. Abingdon: Routledge.

Greenfield, S. (2000) *The Private Life of the Brain*. London: Penguin.

Gregory, E. and Williams, A. (2000) *City Literacies: Learning to Read Across Generations and Cultures*. Abingdon: Routledge.

Gregory, E. and Williams, A. (2004) 'Living literacies in homes and communities', in T. Grainger (ed.), *The RoutledgeFalmer Reader in Language and Literacy*. Abingdon: RoutledgeFalmer.

Hall, C. and Coles, M. (1999) *Children's Reading Choices*. Abingdon: Routledge.

Hall, K. (2003) *Listening to Stephen Read: Multiple Perspectives on Literacy*. Buckingham: Open University Press.

Hall, K. (2004) *Literacy and Schooling: Towards Renewal in Primary Education Policy*. Aldershot: Ashgate.

Hall, K. (2006) 'How children learn to read and how phonics helps', in M. Lewis and S. Ellis (eds), *Phonics, Practice, Research and Policy*. London: Paul Chapman Publishing.

Hall, K. (2009) 'Literacy policy and policy literacy: a tale of phonics in early reading in England', in J. Soler, F. Fletcher-Campbell and G. Reid (eds), *Understanding Difficulties in Literacy Development: Issues and Concepts*. London: Sage.

124

Halliday, M. A. K. (1975) *Learning How to Mean: Explorations in the Development of Language*. London: Edward Arnold.

Hannon, P. (2000) *Reflecting on Literacy in Education*. Abingdon: RoutledgeFalmer.

Hansen, J. (1987) *When Writers Read*. Portsmouth, NH: Heinemann.

Harrison, C. (1999) 'When scientists don't agree: the case for balanced phonics', *Reading*, 33 (2): 59–63.

Hepplewhite, D. (2009) *The Reading Reform Society*. www.rrf.org.uk/. December.

Hughes, T. (1970) 'Myth and education', *Children's Literature in Education*, 1 (1): 12–24.

Hynds, J. (2007) 'Putting a spin on reading: the language of the Rose Review', *Journal of Early Childhood Literacy* (special edition, eds K. Goouch, K. Hall, A. Lambirth and Shannon), 7 (3): 267–81.

Johnston, R. and Watson, L. (2003) *Accelerating Reading and Spelling with Synthetic Phonics: A Five-Year Follow-up*. Edinburgh: Scottish Executive Department, Insight 4.

Johnstone, P. H. (1997) *Knowing Literacy: Constructive Literacy Assessment*. York, ME: Stenhouse Publishers.

Johnstone, P. and Costello, P. (2009) 'Principles for literacy assessment', in F. Fletcher-Campbell, J. Soler and G. Reid (eds), *Approaching Difficulties in Literacy Development: Assessment, Pedagogy and Programmes*. London: Sage.

King, C. and Briggs, J. (2005) *Literature Circles*. Royston: UK Literacy Association.

Kress, G. (1997) *Before Writing: Rethinking the Paths to Literacy*. Abingdon: Routledge.

Lambirth, A. (2007a) 'Social class and the struggle to learn to read: using Bernstein to understand the politics of the teaching of reading', in K. Goouch and A. Lambirth (eds), *Understanding Phonics and the Teaching of Reading: Critical Perspectives*. Maidenhead: Open University Press/McGraw-Hill.

Lambirth, A. (2007b) 'Teachers' voices: talking about children and learning to read', in K. Goouch and A. Lambirth (eds), *Understanding Phonics and the Teaching of Reading: Critical Perspectives*. Maidenhead: Open University Press/McGraw-Hill.

Lambirth, A. and Goouch, K. (2007) 'Golden times of writing: the creative compliance of writing journals', *Literacy, Reading and Language*, 40 (3): 146–52.

Larson, J. and Marsh, J. (2005) *Making Literacy Real: Theories and Practices for Learning and Teaching*. London: Sage.

Lave, J. and Wenger, E. (1991) *Situated Learning: Legitimate Peripheral Participation*. Cambridge: Cambridge University Press.

Lloyd, P. (1990) 'Children's communication', in R. Grieve and M. Hughes (eds), *Understanding Children*. Oxford: Blackwell.

McCallum, I. and Redhead, G. (2000) 'Poverty and educational performance', *Poverty*, 106: 14–17.

McLean, S. V. (1991) *The Human Encounter: Teachers and Children Living Together in Preschools*. Hove: Falmer Press.

McNeil, L. M. (2000) *Contradictions of School Reform: Education Costs of Standardized Tests*. New York: Routledge.

Marshall, B. (1998) 'What they should be learning and how they should be taught', *English in Education*, 32 (1): 4–9.

Medwell, J., Wray, D., Poulson, L. and Fox, R. (1994) *Effective Teachers of Literacy*. Exeter: Exeter University.

Medwell, J., Wray, D., Poulson, L. and Fox, R. (1998) *Effective Teachers of Literacy: A Report of a Research Project Commissioned by the Teacher Training Agency*. Exeter: University of Exeter.

Meek, M. (1982) *Learning to Read*. London: The Bodley Head.

Meek, M. (1987) 'Foreword', in P. Freire and D. Macedo, *Literacy: Reading the Word and the World*. Abingdon: Routledge.

Meek, M. (1988) *How Texts Teach What Readers Learn*. Stroud: Thimble Press.

Meek, M. (1991) *On Being Literate*. London: The Bodley Head.

Messenheimer, T. and Packwood, A. (2002) 'Writing: the state of the state vs. the state of the art in English and American schools', *Reading*, 36 (1): 11–15.

Millard, E. (1997) *Differently Literate: Boys, Girls and the Schooling of Literacy*. Abingdon: Routledge.

Morris, D., Ervin, C. and Conrad, K. (1996) 'A case study of middle school reading disability in teaching struggling readers', *The Reading Teacher*, 49 (5): 368–7.

Morrison, K. and Joan, T. F. H. (2002) 'Testing to destruction: a problem in a small state', *Assessment in Education*, 9: 289–317.

Moss, G. (2005) *Literacy and Gender: Researching Texts, Contexts and Readers*. Abingdon: Routledge.

Moss, P. A. (1998) 'The role of consequences in validity theory', *Educational Measurements: Issues and Practice*, 17 (2): 6–12.

Mullins, I. V. S., Martin, M. O., Kennedy, A. M. and Foy, P. (eds) *PIRLS 2006 International Report: IEA's Progress in International Reading Literacy Study in Primary Schools in 40 Countries*. Available online at: http://timss.bc.edu/pirls2006/intl_rpt.html.

National Strategies (2010) *Assessing Pupils' Progress: A Teacher's Handbook*. London: Crown Publishers.

Noddings, N. (1992) *The Challenge to Care in Schools: An Alternative Approach to Education*. New York: Teachers College Press.

Nutbrown, C. (1996) *Respectful Educators, Capable Learners*. London: Paul Chapman Publishing.

OECD (2009) *PISA 2009 Assessment Framework: Key Competencies in Reading, Mathematics and Science*. OECD Publishing. Online at: www.oecd.org.

Olson, D. (2001) 'Education: the bridge from culture to mind', in D. Bakhurst, and S. G. Shanker (eds), *Jerome Bruner: Language, Culture and Self*. London: Sage.

Perera, K. (1984) *Children's Writing and Reading*. Oxford: Blackwell.

Pinker, S. (1994) *The Language Instinct: How Minds Create Language*. London: Penguin.

Price, C. J. (2000) 'The anatomy of language contributions from functional neuroimaging', *Journal of Anatomy*, 197 (3): 335–9.

Primary National Strategy (2001) *The Primary National Strategy for Literacy*. London: DfEE.

Primary National Strategy (2007) *Letters and Sounds*. Online at: www.standards.dfes.gov.uk/clld/las.html (accessed December 2007).

Radziszewska, B. and Rogoff, B. (1988) 'Influence of adult and peer collaboration on children's planning skills', *Developmental Psychology*, 24: 840–8.

Rex, L. A. and Nelson, M. C. (2004) 'How teachers' professional identities position high-stakes test preparation in their classrooms', *Teachers College Record*, 106: 1288–331.

Rinaldi, C. (2005) 'Documentation and assessment, what is the relationship?', in A. Clark, A. Trine Kjorholt and P. Moss (eds), *Beyond Listening: Children's Perspectives on Early Childhood Services*. Bristol: Policy Press.

Rogoff, B. (1989) 'The joint socialisation of development by young children and adults', in A. Gellatly, D. Rogers and J. Sloboda (eds), *Cognition and Social Worlds*. Oxford: Clarendon Press.

Rogoff, B. (1990) *Apprenticeship in Thinking: Cognitive Development in a Social Context*. New York: Oxford University Press.

Rogoff, B. (2003) *The Cultural Nature of Human Development*. Oxford: Oxford University Press.

Rogoff, B., Goodman-Turkanis, C. and Bartlett (2001) *Learning Together: Children and Adults in a School Community*. Oxford: Oxford University Press.

Rose, J. (2006) *Independent Review of the Teaching of Early Reading*. Nottingham: DfES Publications.

Rosen, M. (2006) 'Synthetic arguments', in M. Lewis and S. Ellis (eds), *Phonics: Practice, Research and Policy*. London: Paul Chapman Publishing.

Sadovnik, A. R. (2001) 'Basil Bernstein (1924–2000): sociologist, mentor and friend', in S. Power, P. Aggleton, J. Brannen, A. Brown, L. Chisholm and J. Mace (eds), *A Tribute to Basil Bernstein 1924–2000*. London: Institute of Education.

Saracho, O. and Spodek, B. (1993) 'Introduction: language and literacy in early childhood education', in B. Spodek and O. Saracho (eds), *Language and Literacy in Early Childhood Education*. New York: Teachers College Press, pp. vii–xiii.

Scott, K. (2010) 'Lost in translation', *Guardian*, 19 January, pp. 1–2.

Shannon, P. (2000) 'A Marxist reading of reading education', *Cultural Logic*, 4 (1).

Shannon, P. (2007) 'The limits of science in the phonics debate', in K. Goouch and A. Lambirth (eds), *Understanding Phonics and the Teaching of Reading*. Maidenhead: Open University Press/McGraw-Hill.

Smith, F. (1973) *Psycholinguistics and Reading*. New York: Holt, Rinehart & Winston.

Smith, F. (1985) *Reading*, 2nd edn. Cambridge: Cambridge University Press.

Smith, G., Smith, T. and Wright, G. (eds) (1997) *Britain Divided: The Growth of Social Exclusion in the 1980s and 1990s*. London: Child Poverty Action Group.

Smith, M. L. (1991) 'Put to the test: the effects of external testing on teachers', *Educational Researcher*, 20 (5): 8–11.

Smith, M. L. and Rottenberg, C. (1991) 'Unintended consequences of external testing in elementary schools', *Educational Measurement: Issues and Practice*, 10 (4): 7–11.

SND (c.1920) *The Songs the Letters Sing*. London and Glasgow: Grant Educational.

Stainthorpe, R. (2006) 'A rose is a rows: a celebration of the importance of accurate word reading to ensure understanding of texts', in M. Lewis and S. Ellis (eds), *Phonics: Practice, Research and Policy*. London: Paul Chapman Publishing.

Stannard, J. (1999) *The National Literacy Strategy*. Keynote speech at UK Reading Association National Conference, 18 March, Cambridge.

Stannard, J. (2006) 'Keeping phonics in perspective', in M. Lewis and S. Ellis (eds), *Phonics: Practice, Research and Policy*. London: Paul Chapman Publishing.

Strauss, S. L. and Altwerger, B. (2007) 'The lographic nature of English alphabetics and the fallacy of direct intensive phonics instruction', in K. Goouch, K. Hall, A. Lambirth and P. Shannon (eds), *Journal of Early Childhood Literacy*, 7 (3): 299–321.

Street, B. V. (1984) *Literacy in Theory and Practice*. Cambridge: Cambridge University Press.

Street, B. V. (1995) *Social Literacies: Critical Approaches to Literacy in Development, Ethnography, and Education*. London: Longman.

Street, B. V. (1996) 'Academic literacies', in J. Clay, D. Baker and C. Fox (eds), *Challenging Ways of Knowing: In English, Mathematics and Science*. Hove: Falmer Press.

Street, B. V. and Street, J. (1991) 'The schooling of literacy', in D. Barton and R. Ivanic (eds), *Writing in the Community*. London: Sage.

Strickland, D. S. and Morrow, L. M. (1990) 'Sharing books' *The Reading Teacher*, 43 (5): 342–3.

Swindal, D. N. (1993) 'The big adventure: using big books for shared reading experiences in the classroom', *The Reading Teacher*, 46 (8): 716–17.

Taylor, M. (1994) 'What children's books tell us about teaching language', in M. E. Bearne, M. Styles and V. Watson (eds), *The Prose and the Passion*. London: Cassell.

Thomas, S. (2000) 'Overall Patterns of Achievement', Working Paper on School Effectiveness. Unpublished.

UK Literacy Association (undated) *Submission to the Review of Best Practice in the Teaching of Early Reading*. Royston: UKLA.

Vygotsky, L. S. (1978) *Mind in Society: The Development of Higher Psychological Processes*. Cambridge, MA: MIT Press.

Vygotsky, L. S. (1986) *Thought and Language*. Cambridge, MA: MIT Press.

Wells, G. (1986) *The Meaning Makers: Children Learning Language and Using Language to Learn*. London: Hodder & Stoughton.

Whitehead, M. (1999) 'A literacy hour in the nursery? The big question mark in *Early Years*', 19 (2): 38–62.

Whitehead, M. (2009) *Supporting Language and Literacy Development in the Early Years*, 2nd edn. Maidenhead: Open University Press/McGraw-Hill.

Winnicott, D. W. (1964) *The Child, the Family and the Outside World*. Harmondsworth: Penguin.

Wood, D. (1988) *How Children Think and Learn*. Oxford: Blackwell.

Woodhead, C. (1995) *A Question of Standards: Finding the Balance*. London: Politiea.

Wray, D. (2006) 'Poor Mr Rose!', in M. Lewis and S. Ellis (eds), *Phonics: Practice, Research and Policy*. London: Paul Chapman Publishing.

Wyse, D. and Goswami, U. (2008) 'Synthetic phonics and the teaching of reading', *British Educational Research Journal*, 34 (6): 691–710.

Wyse, D. and Styles, M. (2007) 'Synthetic phonics and the teaching of reading: the debate surrounding England's "Rose Report"', *Literacy*, 41 (1): 35–42.

Young, M. F. D. (2006) 'Education, knowledge and the role of the state: the "nationalisation" of educational knowledge?', in A. Moore (ed.), *Schooling, Society and Curriculum*. Abingdon: Routledge.

Index